THE ENCYCLOPEDIA OF PSYCHOACTIVE DRUGS

SERIES 1

The Addictive Personality
Alcohol and Alcoholism
Alcohol Customs and Rituals
Alcohol Teenage Drinking
Amphetamines Danger in the Fast Lane
Barbiturates Sleeping Potion or Intoxicant?
Caffeine The Most Popular Stimulant
Cocaine A New Epidemic
Escape from Anxiety and Stress
Flowering Plants Magic in Bloom
Getting Help Treatments for Drug Abuse
Heroin The Street Narcotic
Inhalants The Toxic Fumes

LSD Visions or Nightmares?
Marijuana Its Effects on Mind & Body
Methadone Treatment for Addiction
Mushrooms Psychedelic Fungi
Nicotine An Old-Fashioned Addiction
Over-The-Counter Drugs Harmless or Hazardous?
PCP The Dangerous Angel
Prescription Narcotics The Addictive Painkillers
Quaaludes The Quest for Oblivion
Teenage Depression and Drugs
Treating Mental Illness
Valium and Other Tranquilizers

SERIES 2

Bad Trips
Brain Function
Case Histories
Celebrity Drug Use
Designer Drugs
The Downside of Drugs
Drinking, Driving, and Drugs
Drugs and Civilization
Drugs and Crime
Drugs and Diet
Drugs and Disease
Drugs and Emotion
Drugs and Pain
Drugs and Perception
Drugs and Pregnancy
Drugs and Sexual Behavior

Drugs and Sleep
Drugs and Sports
Drugs and the Arts
Drugs and the Brain
Drugs and the Family
Drugs and the Law
Drugs and Women
Drugs of the Future
Drugs Through the Ages
Drug Use Around the World
Legalization: A Debate
Mental Disturbances
Nutrition and the Brain
The Origins and Sources of Drugs
Substance Abuse: Prevention and Treatment
Who Uses Drugs?

SUBSTANCE ABUSE
PREVENTION
&
TREATMENT

GENERAL EDITOR
Professor Solomon H. Snyder, M.D.

*Distinguished Service Professor of
Neuroscience, Pharmacology, and Psychiatry at
The Johns Hopkins University School of Medicine*

•

ASSOCIATE EDITOR
Professor Barry L. Jacobs, Ph.D.

*Program in Neuroscience, Department of Psychology,
Princeton University*

•

SENIOR EDITORIAL CONSULTANT
Joann Rodgers

*Deputy Director, Office of Public Affairs at
The Johns Hopkins Medical Institutions*

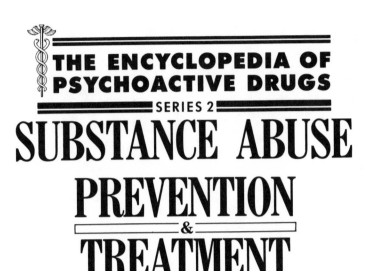

THE ENCYCLOPEDIA OF PSYCHOACTIVE DRUGS
SERIES 2
SUBSTANCE ABUSE
PREVENTION
&
TREATMENT

REGINA AVRAHAM

CHELSEA HOUSE PUBLISHERS
NEW YORK • NEW HAVEN • PHILADELPHIA

EDITOR-IN-CHIEF: Nancy Toff
EXECUTIVE EDITOR: Remmel T. Nunn
MANAGING EDITOR: Karyn Gullen Browne
COPY CHIEF: Juliann Barbato
PICTURE EDITOR: Adrian G. Allen
ART DIRECTOR: Giannella Garrett
MANUFACTURING MANAGER: Gerald Levine

Staff for SUBSTANCE ABUSE: PREVENTION AND TREATMENT

SENIOR EDITOR: Jane Larkin Crain
ASSOCIATE EDITOR: Paula Edelson
ASSISTANT EDITOR: Laura-Ann Dolce
COPY EDITOR: James Guiry
DEPUTY COPY CHIEF: Ellen Scordato
EDITORIAL ASSISTANT: Susan DeRosa
ASSOCIATE PICTURE EDITOR: Juliette Dickstein
PICTURE RESEARCHER: Catherine Ruello
DESIGNER: Victoria Tomaselli
ASSISTANT DESIGNER: Donna Sinisgalli
PRODUCTION COORDINATOR: Joseph Romano
COVER ILLUSTRATION: Mario Ruiz Picture Group

First Printing

1 3 5 7 9 8 6 4 2

Library of Congress Cataloging in Publication Data

Avraham, Regina.
  Substance Abuse: Prevention and Treatment/Regina Avraham

  (The Encyclopedia of Psychoactive Drugs. Series 2)
  Bibliography: p.
  Includes index.
  Juvenile Literature. I. Title. II. Series
  88-4297

ISBN 1-55546-219-7

CONTENTS

An antidrug demonstration in front of the United Nations. The UN's Fund for Drug Abuse Control develops and executes a number of programs to prevent and treat substance abuse problems in many parts of the world.

In the Mainstream
of American Life

One of the legacies of the social upheaval of the 1960s is that psychoactive drugs have become part of the mainstream of American life. Schools, homes, and communities cannot be "drug proofed." There is a demand for drugs — and the supply is plentiful. Social norms have changed and drugs are not only available—they are everywhere.

But where efforts to curtail the supply of drugs and outlaw their use have had tragically limited effects on demand, it may be that education has begun to stem the rising tide of drug abuse among young people and adults alike.

Over the past 25 years, as drugs have become an increasingly routine facet of contemporary life, a great many teenagers have adopted the notion that drug taking was somehow a right or a privilege or a necessity. They have done so, however, without understanding the consequences of drug use during the crucial years of adolescence.

The teenage years are few in the total life cycle, but critical in the maturation process. During these years adolescents face the difficult tasks of discovering their identity, clarifying their sexual roles, asserting their independence, learning to cope with authority, and searching for goals that will give their lives meaning.

Drugs rob adolescents of precious time, stamina, and health. They interrupt critical learning processes, sometimes forever. Teenagers who use drugs are likely to withdraw increasingly into themselves, to "cop out" at just the time when they most need to reach out and experience the world.

Young people learn to use computers at a summer program sponsored by the United Nations. Education, including information about the dangers of drugs, is part of the UN's commitment to the welfare of youth.

Fortunately, as a recent Gallup poll shows, young people are beginning to realize this, too. They themselves label drugs their most important problem. In the last few years, moreover, the climate of tolerance and ignorance surrounding drugs has been changing.

Adolescents as well as adults are becoming aware of mounting evidence that every race, ethnic group, and class is vulnerable to drug dependency.

Recent publicity about the cost and failure of drug rehabilitation efforts; dangerous drug use among pilots, air traffic controllers, star athletes, and Hollywood celebrities; and drug-related accidents, suicides, and violent crime have focused the public's attention on the need to wage an all-out war on drug abuse before it seriously undermines the fabric of society itself.

The anti-drug message is getting stronger and there is evidence that the message is beginning to get through to adults and teenagers alike.

war on drug abuse before it seriously undermines the fabric of society itself.

The anti-drug message is getting stronger and there is evidence that the message is beginning to get through to adults and teenagers alike.

The Encyclopedia of Psychoactive Drugs hopes to play a part in the national campaign now underway to educate young people about drugs. Series 1 provides clear and comprehensive discussions of common psychoactive substances, outlines their psychological and physiological effects on the mind and body, explains how they "hook" the user, and separates fact from myth in the complex issue of drug abuse.

Whereas Series 1 focuses on specific drugs, such as nicotine or cocaine, Series 2 confronts a broad range of both social and physiological phenomena. Each volume addresses the ramifications of drug use and abuse on some aspect of human experience: social, familial, cultural, historical, and physical. Separate volumes explore questions about the effects of drugs on brain chemistry and unborn children; the use and abuse of painkillers; the relationship between drugs and sexual behavior, sports, and the arts; drugs and disease; the role of drugs in history; and the sophisticated drugs now being developed in the laboratory that will profoundly change the future.

Each book in the series is fully illustrated and is tailored to the needs and interests of young readers. The more adolescents know about drugs and their role in society, the less likely they are to misuse them.

Joann Rodgers
Senior Editorial Consultant

THE
SCOVRGE
OF
DRVNKENNES.

By *William Hornby* Gent.

LONDON,
Printed by G. E l d, for *Thomas Baylie*, and are to be solde
at his Shop, in the Middle-Row in Holborne,
neere vnto *Staple-Inne.* 1 6 1 8.

The title page from a 1618 treatise against drunkenness. In the past, alcoholism was regarded as a sign of moral weakness and depravity. Now, however, most experts agree that it is a disease.

INTRODUCTION

The Gift of Wizardry
Use and Abuse

JACK H. MENDELSON, M.D.
NANCY K. MELLO, Ph.D.
Alcohol and Drug Abuse Research Center
Harvard Medical School—McLean Hospital

Dorothy to the Wizard:

"I think you are a very bad man," said Dorothy.
"Oh no, my dear; I'm really a very good man; but I'm a very bad Wizard."
—from THE WIZARD OF OZ

Man is endowed with the gift of wizardry, a talent for discovery and invention. The discovery and invention of substances that change the way we feel and behave are among man's special accomplishments, and, like so many other products of our wizardry, these substances have the capacity to harm as well as to help. Psychoactive drugs can cause profound changes in the chemistry of the brain and other vital organs, and although their legitimate use can relieve pain and cure disease, their abuse leads in a tragic number of cases to destruction.

Consider alcohol — available to all and yet regarded with intense ambivalence from biblical times to the present day. The use of alcoholic beverages dates back to our earliest ancestors. Alcohol use and misuse became associated with the worship of gods and demons. One of the most powerful Greek gods was Dionysus, lord of fruitfulness and god of wine. The Romans adopted Dionysus but changed his name to Bacchus. Festivals and holidays associated with Bacchus celebrated the harvest and the origins of life. Time has blurred the images of the Bacchanalian festival, but the theme of drunkenness as a major part of celebration has survived the pagan gods and remains a familiar part of modern society. The term "Bacchanalian Festival" conveys a more appealing image than "drunken orgy" or "pot party," but whatever the label, drinking alcohol is a form of drug use that results in addiction for millions.

The fact that many millions of other people can use alcohol in moderation does not mitigate the toll this drug takes on society as a whole. According to reliable estimates, one out of every ten Americans develops a serious alcohol-related problem sometime in his or her lifetime. In addition, automobile accidents caused by drunken drivers claim the lives of tens of thousands every year. Many of the victims are gifted young people, just starting out in adult life. Hospital emergency rooms abound with patients seeking help for alcohol-related injuries.

Who is to blame? Can we blame the many manufacturers who produce such an amazing variety of alcoholic beverages? Should we blame the educators who fail to explain the perils of intoxication, or so exaggerate the dangers of drinking that no one could possibly believe them? Are friends to blame — those peers who urge others to "drink more and faster," or the macho types who stress the importance of being able to "hold your liquor"? Casting blame, however, is hardly constructive, and pointing the finger is a fruitless way to deal with the problem. Alcoholism and drug abuse have few culprits but many victims. Accountability begins with each of us, every time we choose to use or misuse an intoxicating substance.

It is ironic that some of man's earliest medicines, derived from natural plant products, are used today to poison and to intoxicate. Relief from pain and suffering is one of society's many continuing goals. Over 3,000 years ago, the Therapeutic Papyrus of Thebes, one of our earliest written records, gave instructions for the use of opium in the treatment of pain. Opium, in the form of its major derivative, morphine, and similar compounds, such as heroin, have also been used by many to induce changes in mood and feeling. Another example of man's misuse of a natural substance is the coca leaf, which for centuries was used by the Indians of Peru to reduce fatigue and hunger. Its modern derivative, cocaine, has important medical use as a local anesthetic. Unfortunately, its increasing abuse in the 1980s clearly has reached epidemic proportions.

The purpose of this series is to explore in depth the psychological and behavioral effects that psychoactive drugs have on the individual, and also, to investigate the ways in which drug use influences the legal, economic, cultural, and even moral aspects of societies. The information presented here (and in other books in this series) is based on many clinical and laboratory studies and other observations by people from diverse walks of life.

Over the centuries, novelists, poets, and dramatists have provided us with many insights into the sometimes seductive but ultimately problematic aspects of alcohol and drug use. Physicians, lawyers, biologists, psychologists, and social scientists have contributed to a better understanding of the causes and consequences of using these substances. The authors in this series have attempted to gather and condense all the latest information about drug use and abuse. They have also described the sometimes wide gaps in our knowledge and have suggested some new ways to answer many difficult questions.

One such question, for example, is how do alcohol and drug problems get started? And what is the best way to treat them when they do? Not too many years ago, alcoholics and drug abusers were regarded as evil, immoral, or both. It is now recognized that these persons suffer from very complicated diseases involving deep psychological and social problems. To understand how the disease begins and progresses, it is necessary to understand the nature of the substance, the behavior of addicts, and the characteristics of the society or culture in which they live.

Although many of the social environments we live in are very similar, some of the most subtle differences can strongly influence our thinking and behavior. Where we live, go to school and work, whom we discuss things with — all influence our opinions about drug use and misuse. Yet we also share certain commonly accepted beliefs that outweigh any differences in our attitudes. The authors in this series have tried to identify and discuss the central, most crucial issues concerning drug use and misuse.

Despite the increasing sophistication of the chemical substances we create in the laboratory, we have a long way to go in our efforts to make these powerful drugs work for us rather than against us.

The volumes in this series address a wide range of timely questions. What influence has drug use had on the arts? Why do so many of today's celebrities and star athletes use drugs, and what is being done to solve this problem? What is the relationship between drugs and crime? What is the physiological basis for the power drugs can hold over us? These are but a few of the issues explored in this far-ranging series.

Educating people about the dangers of drugs can go a long way towards minimizing the desperate consequences of substance abuse for individuals and society as a whole. Luckily, human beings have the resources to solve even the most serious problems that beset them, once they make the commitment to do so. As one keen and sensitive observer, Dr. Lewis Thomas, has said,

> There is nothing at all absurd about the human condition. We matter. It seems to me a good guess, hazarded by a good many people who have thought about it, that we may be engaged in the formation of something like a mind for the life of this planet. If this is so, we are still at the most primitive stage, still fumbling with language and thinking, but infinitely capacitated for the future. Looked at this way, it is remarkable that we've come as far as we have in so short a period, really no time at all as geologists measure time. We are the newest, youngest, and the brightest thing around.

SUBSTANCE ABUSE
PREVENTION
&
TREATMENT

A teenager smokes marijuana. A 1982 survey conducted by the National Institute on Drug Abuse revealed that 20 million Americans were current users of the drug and that some 56 million had used it at least once.

AUTHOR'S PREFACE

Drug addiction has become a public health crisis of major proportions. Although the term *addict* conjures up images of heroin-crazed ghetto dwellers and skid-row winos, the fact is people from all walks of life are susceptible to the lure of mind- and mood-altering drugs. This is true both for legal drugs such as alcohol and nicotine and illegal drugs such as cocaine and heroin.

Because it is legal and its use deeply ingrained in our customs and rituals, alcohol is the drug most widely abused in America. It is estimated that there are between 10 and 13 million alcoholics and problem drinkers in the United States alone.

In the 1980s, cocaine emerged as the major illicit drug of abuse. According to surveys, the number of users in the United States increased by more than one-third between 1982 and 1985, from 4.2 million to 5.8 million. Although one result of the increase in cocaine use was a decline in the heroin addiction rate, the statistics on the abuse of heroin, a highly addictive narcotic, remain alarmingly high. From 1969 to 1974, according to the National Institute on Drug Abuse (NIDA), the number of heroin addicts in the United States more than doubled, from 242,000 to 558,000. Government estimates put the number of heroin addicts in the United States in the mid-1980s at half a million.

First Lady Nancy Reagan greets a group of young people at the White House. They belong to "Just Say No," an organization that helps children fight peer pressure to use drugs.

Addiction exacts a steep price on both the individual victim and society as a whole. It undermines physical and psychological health, leading to chronic illness and sometimes even death. The sizable addict population drains the nation's health care and law enforcement resources, leads to increased crime and violence, and lowers economic productivity.

Clearly, the United States and other nations beset by drug-related woes have a huge stake in preventing addiction from taking hold in the first place and in helping those already mired in substance abuse to recover. Unfortunately, there are enormous profits to be made in supplying the public with psychoactive drugs. This is true for the legitimate alcoholic beverage industry and illicit drug trafficking networks alike. During Prohibition (1920–33), when the 18th Amendment to the Constitution made it illegal to manufacture and sell alcoholic beverages, a lucrative black market developed in their manufacture and distribution. The "experiment that failed," as Prohibition came to be called, more or less proved that legislation cannot prevent a product for which there is a high demand from finding a broad market.

For its part, the illicit drug trade is an international growth industry that thrives on an enormous world demand. It is a highly organized and extremely lucrative business, generating astounding sums of money and showing no signs of diminishing.

Millions of tax dollars have been spent annually in an attempt to disrupt the trade in cocaine and narcotics. These efforts have been an uphill battle and, in many cases, an embarrassing failure. A case in point is the $2.7 million spent in 1985 by the U.S. government to aid antidrug programs in Bolivia. Despite that effort, the United States was unable to eliminate the growth of a single coca plant in that country.

To date, the sale and abuse of drugs continue to plague our society despite the many costly and dangerous attempts that have been made to control them. The economics, politics, and corruption that are part and parcel of the drug trafficking business have set up formidable obstacles to any opposition. Consequently, illegal drugs continue to find their way into our cities, smuggled over our borders and into the hands of those waiting to abuse them.

Because efforts to reduce the supply of illicit drugs are proving unsuccessful, the logical alternative has become reducing the demand for them. This is a matter of raising awareness of the dangers of drug abuse and of finding alternative solutions for people who turn to drugs in an effort to cope with the world around them. It is the purpose of this book to examine the drug problem and the potential that exists for its prevention and treatment. In the chapters that follow we will take a closer look at the roads to addiction that are taken by substance abusers. We will then try to assess why the legal efforts to prevent drugs from reaching the public have failed and explore the steps the government has taken to enter the fields of prevention and treatment. Finally, this book will outline and evaluate the various treatment approaches that have been developed to combat drug abuse and all its consequences.

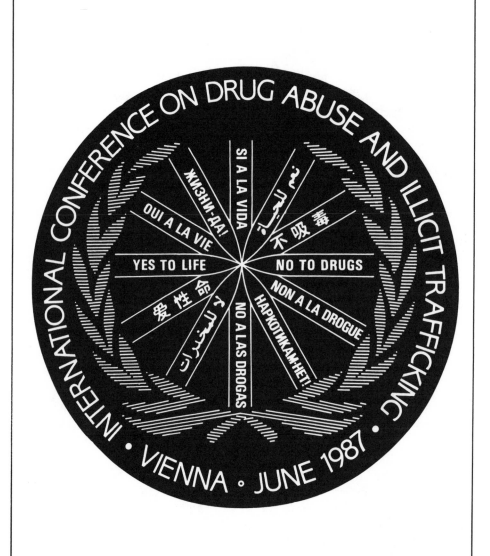

The logo of the 1987 United Nations International Conference on Drug Abuse and Illicit Trafficking. The conference motto, "Yes to Life — No to Drugs," appears in the six official languages of the U.N.

CHAPTER 1

ATTEMPTS AT PREVENTION AND CONTROL

Since the early 1960s, nations across five continents have been engaged in a futile global war against drugs. It has been a consistently escalating war in which the adversaries are grossly mismatched.

On the one side of this conflict are a number of international groups of highly organized drug producers and traffickers. This criminal network has amassed a war chest of billions of dollars in annual profits that gives it the power to corrupt and control a chain of growers, refiners, smugglers, distributors, and dealers. The "enemy" camp also includes an embarrassing number of government officials who cooperate, willingly or otherwise, to strengthen the power of the illegal drug traders.

On the other side of the drug war are the governments whose populations create an enormous demand for drugs. Their weapons are organizations, commissions, bureaus, and agencies. The arsenals are filled with reports, pamphlets, proposals, and slogans. Their front-line attacks are characterized by legislation, treaties, and experimental programs. Often allied with these governments are the mass media and the medical and educational communities. Together, all of these factions combine to wage a losing battle, conceding more and more ground each day. As the war continues, the casualties mount—and society pays the price.

Government and Drug Control

Many governments, witnessing the destruction drugs have brought to their countries, have stepped in with plans of action created to destroy the illegal drug trade. A four-pronged attack used by a number of concerned governments involves crop control, which includes bans on cultivation of illegal crops and reeducation programs; the increased seizure of drug products and financial assets of convicted traffickers; intensified investigation and prosecution of traffickers; and the setting up of programs for effective treatment and prevention of drug abuse.

The first three steps in this attack are the prime responsibilities of governmental agencies. The last step, the effective prevention and treatment of drug abuse, has become the focus of an extensive nationwide effort on the part of health care professionals, educators, legislators, community leaders, and concerned private citizens. We will examine this aspect of the war on drugs more closely in later chapters.

The drug crisis is not limited to any one nation alone, and cooperation among nations is necessary to deal with it. In an address to the United Nations in 1984, John R. Thomas, assistant secretary of state for International Narcotics Matters (INM), referred to the drug problem as "a global menace." In an attempt to encourage cooperative antidrug activities, Secretary Thomas explained that "no nation can cope with drug abuse by relying only on its own treatment, prevention, and domestic enforcement."

To better understand this statement, consider that 80% of the world's cocaine supply is refined in Colombia, from coca paste and coca base smuggled in from Peru and Bolivia. With this fact in mind, it is only natural that the cooperation of Latin American governments would be particularly vital to any international attempt to control the drug trade. And, at first glance, the efforts these governments made in the 1980s to control illicit cultivation appear to be quite commendable.

For example, in 1979 the government of Colombia demonstrated a new "get tough" policy by introducing severe antidrug legislation and signing an extradition treaty for drug traffickers with the United States. In this treaty the Colombian government promised to capture and transport criminals who

A DEA agent stands guard over a haul of cocaine found on a Venezuelan freighter off the coast of West Palm Beach in 1986. South Florida is a major point of entry for illicit drugs into the United States.

were wanted for arrest in the United States. In 1984, the Colombian government sprayed and destroyed 5,000 acres of marijuana plants. That same year, Peru's herbicide eradication program cleared 4,900 acres of coca plants. Mexico, using the same method, reduced its heroin production from 6.5 metric tons in 1975 to 1.4 metric tons in 1983 and also succeeded in reducing its marijuana cultivation.

In other parts of the world, similar efforts have been made to break the hold that drug traders can have on a country. In the early 1980s, Turkey successfully suppressed its opium cultivation and enforced extremely harsh penalties for drug trafficking. The UN Fund for Drug Abuse Control eradicated 10,000 acres of opium poppy cultivation in Thailand and Burma. Long prison terms or death sentences became standard penalties for anyone carrying drugs into such countries as Turkey, Pakistan, and Malaysia.

Despite an enormous outlay of money and manpower, worldwide efforts to stamp out the cultivation of the plants from which illicit drugs are derived have not met with any particular success. In fact, recent research shows that, if anything, the drug traders are gaining momentum.

Why Governments Fail

According to an article in the *New York Times* in August, 1987, more cocaine is flowing out of Colombia than ever before. The world market for cocaine is slightly less than 60 tons. Of that, 40–48 tons are imported to the United States every year. At a fairly steady retail price of $100 a gram, the cocaine trade is an extremely lucrative venture. Considering that the production of cocaine worldwide is in excess of 156 tons, even large seizures by the government would fail to keep drug traders from fulfilling present consumer demand.

The extradition treaty signed by Colombia and the United States was declared unconstitutional by the Colombia Supreme Court in June 1987. This decision is understandable in light of the fact that Colombian law requires the approval

The coffin of Colombian justice minister Rodrigo Lara Bonilla, slain in 1984. He had been zealous in his prosecution of drug traffickers.

Volunteers perform a puppet show in Mexico sponsored by the World Health Organization to alert children to the dangers of drug abuse.

of Supreme Court judges for extradition processes to be carried out and that 13 justices were assassinated in the first 30 months of the treaty's adoption. Where corruption fails, intimidation apparently succeeds; for today, Colombian drug rings control everything from tiny airstrips in Bolivia and Peru to distribution points on American street corners.

Antidrug campaigns have been effectively neutralized by the wealth and violence of drug rings. In 1984 the Colombian minister of justice, a strong advocate of antinarcotic controls, was machine-gunned to death on a Bogota street. In late 1986, a prominent Colombian newspaper editor who had criticized the drug bosses was murdered.

Corruption and fear have taken their toll in other countries, as well. They have left the Mexican antidrug programs on the verge of failure, resulting in a marked increase in Mexican heroin, marijuana, and cocaine on the U.S. drug market. Colombian cocaine processing centers have been discovered in Panama and among tribal groups in the jungles of Brazil. In the Far East, the drug trade moves from countries that hamper its movements to others that welcome a share of its profits. Opium trafficking, for example, has moved from Pakistan to Afghanistan. The drug trade recently has become a major source of financing for terrorist groups in several nations and has found support and sanctuary throughout the world.

The situation within the borders of the United States does not present any more encouraging a picture. The United States is a market for more than two-thirds of all cocaine distributed in the world. The year 1987 brought a resurgence of heroin use in New York, the center of the narcotics market. Heroin had been on a steady decline since the early 1980s but is once again striving for a competitive portion of the drug trade.

Marijuana has become a major cash crop on the farmlands of America. In California, marijuana is grown commercially in 43 of the state's 58 counties. In Kentucky and Oklahoma, marijuana cultivation brings in a combined total of $400 million each year. Ironically, the serious cultivation of marijuana in the United States began in 1978, when the Mexican government dusted the marijuana crop with paraquat, a lung-damaging herbicide. American growers soon learned that home production was a lot less risky than smuggling.

Sadly, we are at present in a state of siege. The populations of many countries are being held hostage by drug producers and traffickers. The people of the United States are in no less a vulnerable condition than are the people of other nations. As Lester Wolff, former chairman of the House Select Committee on Narcotics Abuse and Control, recently stated, "The federal government has declared so many wars on drugs that if we lost that many wars the U.S. wouldn't be around."

Why Laws Fail

In most parts of the world, and certainly in the United States, it is illegal to produce, distribute, purchase, or possess most psychoactive drugs (other than alcohol and nicotine) without a license or prescription. Some states have repealed or reduced criminal penalties for minor possession or use of marijuana, but strong legislation against narcotics and cocaine is standard. Yet drug use and drug trafficking increase steadily. The lawmakers have been unable to make a dent in the drug crisis.

Part of the problem lies in the way in which drugs are classified under the law. The most abused drug in use today is alcohol, which is classified as a legal drug and can be purchased in any amount by any adult. Antialcohol legislation places minor restrictions on when and where alcohol may be sold or imbibed. Killing another person with a vehicle while intoxicated is still classified as an accident in some states while killing someone with a knife while under the influence of PCP is classified as murder.

Interestingly, marijuana, a drug derived from the hemp plant, is legally considered a narcotic (any substance that sedates, has a depressant effect, and/or causes dependence), which it technically is not. Similarly, cocaine, a stimulant, is also subject to the Narcotics Control Act. The law seems to

A U.S. Customs officer inspects the 957 pounds of cocaine seized in a 1984 drug bust off the coast of Florida. The United States is a market for more than two-thirds of the world's supply of cocaine.

A Kennedy Airport employee covers his face after being arrested for his participation in a cocaine smuggling ring. The ring, which counted 40 members and was thought to have handled $1.5 billion in cocaine, was broken up by federal agents in 1987.

have been remiss in examining the individual nature of drugs and in classifying them in a way that is meaningful to the public.

Drug laws today are going the way of Prohibition legislation. As did the antialcohol amendment, harsher laws and enforcement against drug suppliers are serving to assist rather than suppress the drug trade. It appears that stricter law enforcement results in higher street prices of drugs. Unlike other markets, the demand for drugs is not controlled by price. As drug prices rise, users commit more crimes to pay for them. The facts lead some people to conclude that harsher drug laws cause more, not less, crime.

Another reason that the law has failed is that it does not recognize the nature of drug addiction. The fear of imprisonment will never cause an addict to stop using a drug. He cannot make a simple choice to end a drug dependency, for his body will not allow him to do so — it needs the drug, and an abrupt withdrawal can cause severe pain and even death.

A local artist painted this childlike warning against crack on the side of a public school building in New York City. An adulterated form of cocaine, crack is the most addictive drug on the streets.

by the Board of Education amounted to one afternoon during which all teachers were required only to watch a film about this drug.

In short, drug education, with its lack of emphasis on teacher training and its incorrect data, has succeeded only in giving lip service to any significant methods of drug prevention.

Prevention and the Media

During the past few years, the media — radio, television, films, magazines, and newspapers — have attempted to participate in drug prevention. There has been a concerted effort on the part of the media to warn young people to "say no to drugs." Public-service announcements and programs keep the dangers of drug use in the forefront of public attention, and news broadcasts keep the viewers aware of drug-related deaths and crime.

However, by emphasizing that drug abuse is a problem of our youth culture, the media antidrug policy virtually dic-

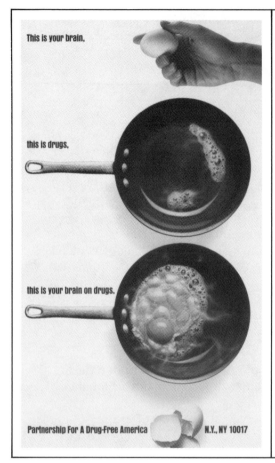

This is your brain,

this is drugs,

this is your brain on drugs.

Partnership For A Drug-Free America   N.Y., NY 10017

A poster published by Partnership for a Drug-Free America. Opinion is split on the effectiveness of such graphic statements. Some people feel hard-hitting and uncompromising antidrug warnings are the best way to get the message across. Others maintain that sensationalism of any kind serves only to glamorize drug use.

tated a route for rebellion. By publicizing drugs that were not even available in many communities, radio and television programs informed an entire generation of young people about the broad range of mind-altering drugs from which they could choose. For many students, warnings about drugs served as lures. The 1972 Consumers Union Report on Licit and Illicit Drugs states that publicizing the horrors of the "drug menace" tends to popularize many drugs. The report claims that sensationalist publicity is not only ineffective but counterproductive.

The mass media often act as a mirror of the values of society. Television commercials tell people that there is always something to take if they feel down. Social drinking is regularly shown as a way to enhance conviviality, relax, or cope with stress. Illicit drugs are shown in hundreds of sensationalized, glamorous dramas that may cause many a youngster to ask "What am I missing?" At the same time, the scare tactics employed in exciting, fictionalized settings are normally discarded as just "part of the show" by a very experienced viewing public.

At the present time, it would appear that neither governments, laws, nor educational programs are making any inroads into the drug trade. Drug traffic is increasing; drug abuse is growing.

When prevention fails and drugs inevitably flow into the country, the only option left open is to treat the subsequent addiction. In order to successfully do this, however, it is first necessary to understand what addiction is, what it does to the addict, and who is vulnerable to it.

Cigarette manufacturers are required by law to print labels on each package alerting consumers to the health hazards of smoking. Nicotine is among the most addictive of all psychoactive drugs.

CHAPTER 2

THE NATURE OF ADDICTION

In everyday terms, an addiction is a compulsive need for a particular substance or activity. People who are addicted depend on these things to get along in their daily lives. They give in, day after day, to a very strong craving that needs to be satisfied. Millions of people are trapped in addictions they scarcely recognize. An uncontrollable urge for sugar is labeled as a "sweet tooth," and a serious need for caffeine is disguised as a pleasant "coffee break."

Consider how many millions of people remain addicted to nicotine, even as they openly acknowledge the serious risk that cigarette smoking presents to health. Think about the many others who are uncontrollably addicted to gambling, to overspending on credit cards, or to living as "workaholics." Addictions of any sort are destructive in that they deprive the addict of the ability to exercise control over his or her life. By definition, an addiction offers no choice to the addict and often is the direct cause of serious disruption in the person's health or life-style.

The most serious addictions of all involve psychoactive drugs. These substances radically alter the user's mind and body, undermining health, economic stability, and social functioning. It is this form of addiction and abuse that most immediately threatens all of society.

The Substances of Abuse

The U.S. Drug Enforcement Administration (DEA) recognizes some 100 separate illicit substances as being abused by significant numbers of people. Alcohol, a legal drug, is not included among these substances but must be included in any examination of substances that are addictive and highly destructive to both their users and society as a whole.

The major substances of abuse and addiction that will be considered in this discussion are as follows:

Narcotics: These include heroin, morphine, codeine, opium, and methadone. Narcotics are painkillers and cause both drowsiness and a sense of euphoria, or extreme well-being.

A display of marijuana and the paraphernalia used to smoke it.

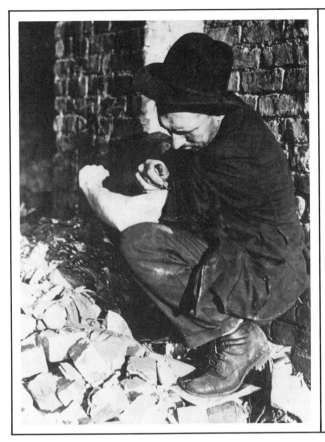

A derelict injects himself with heroin. In the late 1980s, intravenous drug users are the main transmitters of the AIDS virus among heterosexuals.

Depressants: These include barbiturates, methaqualone (Quaaludes), and minor tranquilizers such as Valium and Librium. Depressants act to slow down the body's central nervous system, thereby acting as relaxants that are both calming and sleep inducing.

Stimulants: These include cocaine, crack, and amphetamines. Stimulants speed up the activities of the central nervous system and increase alertness and energy levels as they bring about a state of euphoria.

Hallucinogens: These include LSD, PCP (angel dust), and mescaline. Hallucinogens cause hallucinations, illusions, and distortions of the senses.

Cannabis: These include marijuana and hashish. Cannabis drugs cause changes in mood, mental functioning, and feelings, as they bring on a state of euphoria.

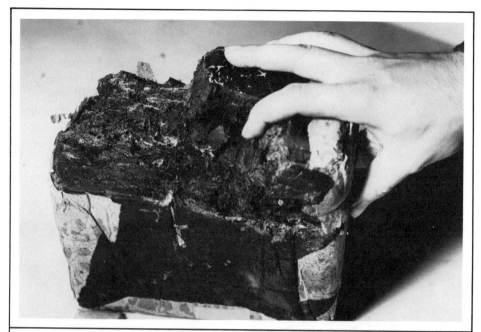

A sample of opium produced in Pakistan. Opium's calming, painkilling, and sleep-inducing properties were first recognized more than 4,000 years ago. So, too, was its powerful addictive property.

Whatever the drug of choice, all are potentially addictive substances that, over time, can cause psychological and physiological dependence in the user. The time that separates casual drug use and addiction ranges dramatically according to the individual substance. For example, crack use can result in severe physical dependence after only one or two uses; cocaine addiction may take several years to develop.

Addiction and the Body

All addictions in some way affect body processes. As a given substance acts on the blood, the brain, and the central nervous and glandular systems, the chemistry of the body becomes gradually and subtly altered. The user's dependent craving for a drug usually sets in once the chemical balance of the body has become significantly changed by that drug. It is at this point that the user begins to take the drug because he or she needs, rather than actually wants, it.

When an addictive substance is introduced, the body's organs build defenses against the intruder. As a result of these physical changes, the body builds up a tolerance and attempts to become accustomed to the new substance. Tolerance to a drug causes more and more of the substance to be needed to achieve the same effect. This is what prompts the addict to take ever higher doses. And so, the cycle is self-perpetuating: the need, the drug, the pleasure, the tolerance, the increase in dosage, the addiction.

Once a user has become accustomed to a drug and developed a need for it, abrupt cessation of drug taking results in a withdrawal syndrome. Symptoms can include severe physical pain, tremors, sweating, psychological disturbance, convulsions, and in some extreme cases, death.

Who Becomes an Addict?

James M. is an alcoholic. He must have his quota of drinks every day. He drinks before he leaves for work, throughout the day from a bottle of liquor he keeps in his desk drawer at the office, and again in the evening. He is unable to go anywhere without the assurance that a drink is within easy reach. James rarely becomes noticeably drunk, but times are few and far between when he is fully sober.

James began drinking regularly as a teenager, but his problem became more serious a few years ago, when he had difficulties coping with the pressures of a new job and things started going wrong at home. A few drinks with the "boys" had always helped James to relax, but then James discovered that a few more drinks helped him to forget his problems entirely for a while. In the beginning, he seldom, if ever, drank alone. And yet none of James's fellow drinkers became alcoholics. Some of them even drank more than James did in any one evening. Then why did James become an alcoholic? Why, out of all of the friends who drank with him, was he the one to become an addict?

It is still unknown why some people become addicted to drugs while others do not. Despite all the research that has been done, there are very few definite answers. However, there are several theories about the causes of drug addiction. Some studies have shown possible biochemical links to alcoholism, which suggests that some people have allergies that act as a protection against this disorder. Genetic studies of children of alcoholics have lent strong support to the theory that alcoholism (as well as other addictions) is an inherited condition. One theory on alcohol addiction was advanced as early as 1946 by Dr. E. M. Jellinek, a pioneer researcher and theorist on alcohol-related disorders, who viewed alcoholism as an illness and not the behavior of choice of undesirable people. Today it is widely understood that alcoholism is indeed an illness.

Dr. Forrest S. Tennant, former executive director of Community Health Projects in California, believes that all addictions are chronic, recurring diseases that strike otherwise healthy people. On the other hand, the studies conducted by Dr. Nils Bejerat of the Karolinska Institute in Stockholm focused on the substance rather than the person. Dr. Bejerat remains convinced that anyone can become addicted if given an addictive substance over a period of time.

Young men enjoying their last legal drink in New York State on November 30, 1985. The next day, New York and 31 other states raised the legal drinking age to 21. This is one of several measures being instituted across the country to combat drunk driving.

Other studies indicate that people who become addicts have underlying psychological disorders. These studies conclude that most addicts had major disturbances during childhood. Dr. Lawrence J. Hatterer of New York Hospital-Cornell Medical Center relates all addiction to excessive neglect by one or both parents. He feels that the addiction is a method by which the addicts hurt themselves as a reaction to this mistreatment.

Dr. Janice Keller Phelps, a specialist in the treatment of addiction, has developed a theoretical working model to help her treat addicts. This model is based on the premise that all addictions are physiological in origin. Dr. Phelps claims that addiction arises from metabolic mistakes built into the biochemistry of each addict (much like the metabolic flaw in diabetics, which causes excess sugar in the blood and urine). This chemical error is then passed down genetically and leaves the individual vulnerable to a wide variety of addictive substances.

Although there is still no real evidence to support a single, definite cause for addiction, there are some factors that many experts agree on. It seems apparent that people who cannot reach a state of mind that they desire by ordinary means seek an artificial solution by turning to drugs. Drugs can serve to relieve a sense of powerlessness for a short period of time.

It has also been determined that the choice of drugs is usually determined by several factors, including the person's personality, his or her financial status, his or her opportunity to buy a given drug, the drug's availability, and by social custom and manner of living.

The experts also agree that, whatever the addiction, the end results are not only serious bodily harm but serious personality defects: the loss of self-respect, self-esteem, and self-confidence and the growth of a deep and painful self-hatred.

Recognizing Addiction

Most addicts adamantly deny to themselves and to others that they are addicted. Often they are convinced that they can stop their substance abuse at will. As the addiction becomes more controlling and as they become more aware of their dependence, addicts often begin to go to great lengths to conceal their conditions.

Dr. Forest Tennant (left) with National Football League Commissioner Pete Rozelle during a 1986 press conference to announce the NFL's new drug-testing program. Tennant, who is in charge of the program, believes that drug addiction is a chronic illness to which even psychologically healthy people can become vulnerable once they expose themselves to addictive substances.

Family members can sometimes contribute to the denial of addiction by closing their eyes to what are often clear signals that something is very wrong. Acknowledging the addiction of a close friend or relative is a painful experience, but the first step in any attempt to help a drug user is recognizing the signs of possible addiction.

Here are some questions to ask yourself if you suspect that someone you know may be abusing drugs:

1. Are there any major changes in behavior: Is the person more irritable than usual? Does he or she have "temper tantrums"? Is there unusual indifference or apathy?
2. Does the person want to be alone more than usual? Does he or she spend inordinate amounts of time isolated from the rest of the family?

3. Does the person spend more time away from home?
4. Does the person have a great deal more or less money than one would expect?
5. Are there phone calls at odd hours?
6. Are there major changes in friends?
7. Is there a dramatic change of performance on the job or at school?
8. Is there money missing from the house?
9. Has there been a change in energy levels: listlessness, fatigue, etc.?
10. Has there been a dramatic change in eating habits?

Of course, none of these signals, in isolation, suggests that anyone is addicted to drugs. However, if the answer to a number of these questions is "yes," it would be wise to consider the possibility that drugs may be part of the picture. If this is the case, the next step should certainly be treatment of the drug addiction.

An artist's rendering of the suffering caused by alcoholism. Alcoholics Anonymous, started in 1935, is by far the most successful treatment program for this disease and serves as a model for many other approaches.

CHAPTER 3

TREATING DRUG ABUSE

Until very recently, the drug abuser was looked upon as a degenerate with weak moral character and low moral values. He was someone to be shunned, or perhaps pitied. Those professions in which drug use was thought to be widespread were regarded with varying degrees of disapproval. People in the arts—musicians, actors, painters, and writers—traditionally were viewed as a class apart from the mainstream of society, at least in part because such types held unconventional views about the use of drugs—alcohol and marijuana in particular.

Communities everywhere have tolerated a certain amount of alcohol intoxication, made fun of their town drunk, or kept a "drunk tank" in the local jail for sobering up. Until the late 1960s, however, when widespread drug use began to spread from the ghettos and from the artistic communities into society at large, most people knew little and cared less about the realities of substance abuse.

A Brief History

To be sure, the medical community had witnessed addiction to alcohol, morphine, and opium among patients prior to the 20th century. Addiction to morphine goes back to the Civil War, when it was used as a painkiller in the treatment of

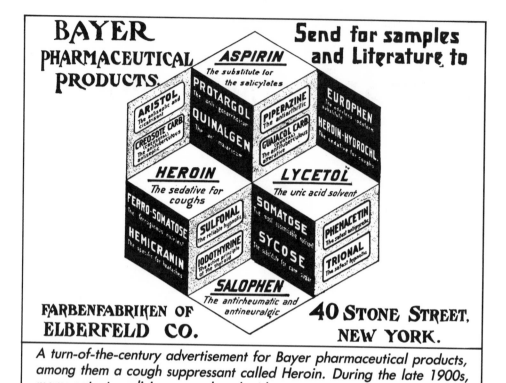

A turn-of-the-century advertisement for Bayer pharmaceutical products, among them a cough suppressant called Heroin. During the late 1900s, many patent medicines were laced with opiates and alcohol.

wounded soldiers. During the 19th century, opium and its chief active ingredient, morphine, were sold openly in grocery and general stores and through the mail in patent medications. No wonder, then, that many people became chemically dependent on these narcotics, which were as available to the public then as aspirin is today.

During the 19th century, however, the user of opiates was not considered in any way menacing or disreputable. People also failed to recognize that America's habituation to the hard drugs found in the various elixirs and patent medicines touted as cure-alls by their purveyors constituted a drug "epidemic" in its own right.

By the beginning of the 20th century, however, medical professionals and law enforcement officials alike had come to the realization that the unregulated buying and selling of potentially dangerous drugs could not go on unchecked. Hoping to correct the situation, in 1906 Congress passed the

Pure Food and Drug Act, which required labels on all medicines to state clearly the alcohol, narcotic (heroin and all derivatives of opium), and cocaine contents. In 1914, Congress passed the Harrison Narcotics Act. This law required anyone who imported, manufactured, or sold narcotics (cocaine was mislabeled as a narcotic) to register with the government and pay a special tax.

Under the terms of the Harrison Act, physicians were still permitted to prescribe opiates as medicine but were forbidden to dispense any morphine or opium to people who were addicted. To help those who had become addicted to these substances, the federal government established 44 maintenance clinics throughout the country that supplied addicts with legal drugs.

These clinics were by no means treatment centers. They were set up in an attempt to control the importation and sale of narcotics rather than to confront the problems of addicts.

A woodcut portrays an operation performed by an army surgeon during the Civil War. Morphine was prescribed so freely for pain during this war that its overuse became known as the "soldier's disease."

Unfortunately, one consequence of this legislation was the beginning of an organized network of dope smugglers and peddlers who carried on a profitable "underground" trade through Mexico and Canada. At that point, heroin also began to enter the country in significant amounts, and 20 cities in the United States reported that more people were using narcotics after the Harrison Act was passed than had used them before. By 1925, all the maintenance clinics in the country had been closed.

In the 1930s, the federal government made another attempt to stem the growing use of drugs and set up two drug treatment hospitals. The first hospital was established in Lexington, Kentucky, in 1935; the second, in Fort Worth, Texas, in 1938. Both of these institutions were designed to help drug users overcome addictions through detoxification programs. These programs, however, were largely unsuccessful at keeping addicts from returning to drug use once they were released from the hospital.

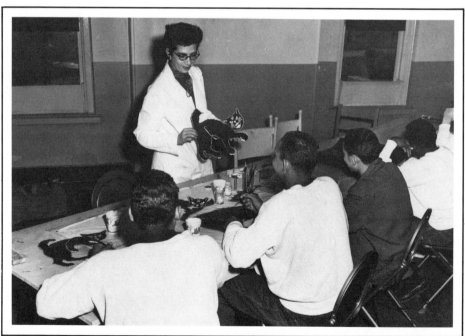

A 1952 occupational therapy class at Riverside Hospital in New York City, the first drug treatment facility exclusively for juvenile addicts.

In 1939, a historic step in the treatment of addiction took place with the publication of Bill Wilsons's *Alcoholics Anonymous*. This unprecedented book presented an entirely new approach to the treatment of alcoholism and continues to serve as a model for the treatment of all drug addictions today.

During the 1950s, a number of developments signaled a growing awareness of the need for new approaches to the treatment of drug addiction. Riverside Hospital in New York City became the first drug treatment facility to treat juvenile addicts exclusively. And in 1958, an important breakthrough occurred when Chuck Dederich, a former member of Alcoholics Anonymous (AA), introduced the treatment center concept.

Synanon, the first such treatment center, was set up to reach out to those whom all existing treatment facilities had failed. It was, and still is today, a residential treatment program designed to provide the addict with communal support to help him overcome addiction.

By the mid 1960s and 1970s there was no longer any question as to the serious nature of drug abuse, and hundreds of different treatment programs began to spring up around the country. Experimental inpatient and outpatient programs were introduced by city, state, and federal agencies, medical groups, schools, churches, and private organizations. Free telephone hot lines, such as 1-800-COCAINE, were established to provide immediate information and help for addicts. Self-help groups and street walk-in programs joined the ranks of treatment and rehabilitation approaches that were available for the growing numbers of drug abusers.

By the early 1980s, seeking treatment for chemical dependency had become an acceptable and commendable step, taken publicly by many well-known people. In 1982, former first lady Betty Ford established a treatment center in her name in Mirage, California. Mrs. Ford had courageously admitted to the American people that she had overcome an alcohol and drug dependency.

Today the need for treatment of drug addictions is recognized and supported by most experts. Although the success rate of the different treatment programs is nowhere near its goal, what matters most is that help is available to, and reaching, significant numbers of people who desperately need it.

Methods of Treatment

The oldest and most successful treatment program in the world is that of AA. It is based on a self-help concept, run by alcoholics for alcoholics. The AA method has been incorporated into many present-day treatment centers, and large numbers of cocaine and heroin addicts are now turning to AA for help. (The philosophy and methodology of AA will be examined in detail in Chapter 5.)

Other current methods of helping people addicted to both alcohol and other drugs range from short-term outpatient programs to long-term inpatient treatment. Some help is temporary, designed to help the addict through crisis periods; other programs are concerned with changing the drug user's lifelong and ingrained pattern of self-destruction.

Every major city offers addicts a place to turn. Such a place might be a storefront facility that is open 24 hours a day or a church or school program where counselors are available for a few hours a week. It might be the drug-abuse center of a local hospital or the intervention expert at the other end of a telephone hot line.

The type of help available at short-term facilities is often free to anyone in need. These centers offer information and often hold group therapy and individual counseling sessions conducted by psychiatrists or physicians. Some centers concentrate on methods of coping with problems and teach stress-relief techniques such as meditation and yoga. Others teach the addict how to say no and how to find alternatives to drugs.

The more intensive methods of treatment, which are designed to separate the user from his drug of choice, fall into three main categories: detoxification programs, maintenance programs, and residential treatment centers. Each of these programs is quite different in intent and approach from the other two.

Three Major Treatment Programs

Detoxification is used to get a person off alcohol and/or other drugs as quickly as possible. To detoxify means to rid the body of poisons or their effect. Detoxification attempts to relieve the addict, in as short a time as possible, of the agony

Workers staff a drug abuse hot line at Fair Oaks Hospital in New Jersey, a residential psychiatric facility known for its pioneering work in the treatment of addiction.

of physiological and psychological withdrawal. Those who apply this method believe that the detoxified addict will be better able to abstain from further use of the drug.

A person undergoing detoxification will go "cold turkey." That is, he or she will be required suddenly to stop any use of the addicting substance. There will be no slow tapering off, only an abrupt end to any contact with the drug. Some detoxification programs provide medication to ease the difficulties related to withdrawal. These might be minor tranquilizers, Clonidine (which binds to opiate receptors in the brain, thus preventing the opiates from doing so), or naltrexone, a medication that will prevent the user from experiencing any euphoria, or high, that a drug may induce.

Most detoxification is done on an outpatient basis, although some patients require hospitalization. The entire treatment period is three weeks or less. Most people in these programs are able to rid their bodies of a drug for a period of time. Unfortunately, and possibly because no psychological help is included in this sort of program, the average addict who has been detoxified returns to drug use within two weeks.

Maintenance is a program used primarily in cases of heroin addiction. The heroin user is given methadone, a synthetic narcotic, by mouth. Methadone satisfies the addict's need for a narcotic without supplying the effects that keep the user from functioning in his or her daily life.

Methadone must be taken every 24 hours. It leaves the user feeling "normal" rather than "high" and costs a fraction of the amount needed to support an illicit heroin habit. A year's supply of methadone can be administered for about $2,000. On methadone, the addict usually can hold a job, relate to others, and avoid turning to crime to pay for street heroin.

As might be expected, there are a number of problems associated with methadone maintenance. First, methadone must be taken every day. Although a new synthetic narcotic, LAAM, has been developed as a methadone substitute, with the advantage that its duration of action is two to three days, both drugs require an enormous commitment on the part of the patient in order to be effective. There can be no break in the treatment, and as a result, the methadone user actually has exchanged one addiction for another.

Another problem with maintenance is that about 25 percent of methadone users turn to alcohol to satisfy the need for a high. The mixture of methadone and alcohol is a highly dangerous combination and accounts for many deaths each year.

The methadone maintenance program has many critics. The program, which has its practical advantages, accepts the condition of addiction. Its supporters claim success in achieving the program's main purpose: relieving both the addict and society at large of the most negative aspects of heroin addiction. However, its critics are deeply concerned about a treatment approach that in effect substitutes one addiction for another. The increasing controversy over methadone maintenance will be examined more closely in Chapter 6.

Residential treatment centers service thousands of drug abusers throughout the country. Some treatment centers are situated in lovely, scenic settings; others are found in crowded inner cities. They vary in size from 35- to 500-bed facilities and have a wide range of fees, depending on the services offered.

Of the more than 300 treatment centers in the United States, most are based on a 24-hour community program. The communal support given to patients in the facility is aimed at permanently changing lifelong patterns of destructive behavior. Some centers insist that patients stay in residential treatment for at least 15 months before they try to return to the outside world. Others have intensive programs that last from one to nine months. In some situations, addicts "graduate" to halfway houses, where they live together for further support before going out on their own.

Treatment may vary from center to center, depending on the specific addictions and type of addict being dealt with. However, there is a traditional routine that characterizes most

I WAS THE VICE PRESIDENT OF A FORTUNE 500 COMPANY.

I had a beautiful family, a big house in the suburbs, everything I wanted. Then I got into cocaine and I almost lost it all. It's a lie that cocaine's not addictive. I didn't choose to be an addict. Quitting cocaine was the only thing I couldn't do by myself. I'll be a recovering addict day by day for the rest of my life.

COCAINE. THE BIG LIE. CALL 1-800-662-HELP.

The essential first step in treating addiction is for the victim to admit that he or she has a problem and needs help. This poster is aimed at business executives and other fast-track types, many of whom have a particular vulnerability to cocaine.

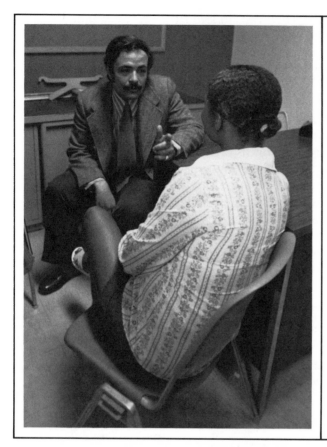

A counselor at a New York City methadone program talks with an in-patient. Most experts agree that psychotherapy is necessary to the success of methadone maintenance programs that treat heroin addiction.

centers, and experience has shown that these centers have had the greatest impact on addiction.

The primary staff members at a treatment center are nondegreed professionals. These people, who serve both clinical and custodial roles, are former drug addicts or alcoholics who have been rehabilitated in a treatment-center program. This practice follows through on the belief that only former addicts can truly understand and break through the lies and denials that are part of an addict's behavior. In fact, many treatment centers also prefer that their degreed staff — the doctors, nurses, psychiatrists, educators, and even administrators—be rehabilitated addicts.

Activities at treatment centers are designed to work a complete change in the addict's life-style. They are part of a highly structured schedule, with strict timetables that cover every minute of the day. The addict may be involved in group therapy, personal counseling, learning sessions, formal education classes, and regularly assigned residential chores. Every activity is geared to promote within the addict a complete abstinence from drugs and a sense of self-reliance and personal honesty.

One problem with residential treatment has been keeping the addict in the program long enough to effect a significant change. Predictably, studies show that those who stay longer fare better after they leave the program than do those who have a shorter stay. Nevertheless, treatment centers are a most optimistic option for thousands of people whose lives have been disrupted and destroyed by drugs.

A mother at a residential facility in Pennsylvania for women convicts. She is a recovering addict who was able to complete her high school education while in detention.

CHAPTER 4

ADDICTION AND THE FAMILY

Alcoholics and drug abusers do not live in isolation. Their lives are intertwined with those of others, all of whom — friends, family members, fellow students, and co-workers — are seriously affected by the problems that accompany addiction. Drug use by its very nature disrupts family life, alienates close friends and relatives, and leaves deep and often permanent scars on those who live in its midst.

On the other hand, the different members of an addict's family also play a very significant role in the life of a drug user. They may act as the support system that helps to rescue the addict from total ruin or as the unwitting instrument that drives him more deeply down the path of self-destruction.

The relationships in any family setting that includes a drug abuser are sensitive and complex. Understanding what happens to families touched by drug addiction is an important part of understanding how drug-related problems may be treated. To further this understanding, we will try to examine some of the dynamics that take place between drug abusers and the people who are close to them.

Youngsters learning to read at a day-care center. The children of addicts are the truly innocent victims of drug abuse, because they rarely get the kind of nurturing they need early in life.

Facing the Problem

Alan, at 19, was already a veteran "cokehead." He had been using cocaine for more than a year and was dealing the drug in order to help pay for his own supply. In the last few months Alan had "graduated" to crack and now was hopelessly hooked. Although Alan's mother felt in her heart that something about Alan had changed — that something was wrong — she said nothing. She explained things to herself by saying that young men change as they grow into adulthood, and after all, it was only two years since his father had passed away.

It was evident that Alan was no longer the active, on-the-go youngster he had been during his first few years in high school. He was not home very much anymore, and when he was, he was either moody and irritable or isolated behind the closed door of his room. His old friends were not coming around anymore, and strange voices over the telephone asked for Alan at odd hours of the day and night. Still, his mother said nothing.

It was only when Alan started stealing money from her wallet that her suspicions reached a pitch she could no longer ignore. She finally confronted him. An unusually abusive and enraged Alan swore at his mother and denied taking any money. He shouted that he was old enough to do as he pleased and that he only did drugs when he was down and needed to feel better. As she heard Alan slam the door behind him, his mother felt that her world had just come to an end. Her only son was on drugs, and there was nothing at all that she could do about it.

Scenes similar to this are repeated over and over in thousands of homes. The characters and the dialogue change, but all over the country family and friends continue to discover that someone they live with is involved with drugs. Sometimes, as in the case of Alan's mother, the suspicion has been there for a long time. At other times, the discovery comes as a sudden shock. Whatever the case, it is always a painful moment of truth, but it is in no way, as Alan's mother felt, the end of the world.

There is no manual of instructions for addressing drug use, no tried-and-true response that will result in an instant solution. However, it is possible to learn how certain actions and attitudes may be very helpful when dealing with a family member or friend who is in trouble with drugs. It is also possible to become aware of those responses that may make the problem worse and create an even greater rift between the drug user and his family.

A first step in facing the problem of drug abuse is to develop a greater sense of reality about the typical home in modern society. The average home is a storehouse of addictive substances. Where is the home that is free of all caffeine, tobacco, alcoholic beverages, tranquilizers, and sleeping pills? Where is the family that sets the ideal example for all of its members?

The reality is that young people learn very early in life that many others around them are regular, often habitual, users of many addictive chemicals. Another reality is that almost all young people will, at some time in their lives, experiment with some form of drug. They may smoke cigarettes, drink some alcohol, or become curious about a prescription pill they find in the family medicine chest. Or they may try marijuana or experiment with cocaine.

Fortunately, most people who experiment with drugs do not become addicts. However, knowing this is no reason to accept the casual use of drugs. The family that is informed, that understands the effects and hazards of drug use, is far ahead of the game. And though an awareness that a family member has tried drugs is not a time for overreaction or panic, it is a time for family concern.

Honestly confronting the issue of drug use is the responsibility of all members of the family. When members of a family can talk openly about drugs, there is less danger of their abuse. When the problems of any one member of a family become the problems of all, the danger decreases even more.

Still, drug addiction can come to the best of families. Even where communication is free and trust is strong, drug abuse may be lurking in the shadows. How often has the parent of a drug user boasted, "Not *my* child!" Unfortunately, it can be your child, your sister or brother, your parent, your spouse, your friend. Where drugs are concerned, no one is immune, and denial is no solution.

Dealing with the Problem

If one member of a family does become involved with drugs, the most important step to take may also be the most difficult one. This involves becoming objective and detached from the problem. It is not easy to be unemotional about the addiction of someone who is a part of one's life. It is very human to wonder, "Where have I gone wrong?" or "How could you do this to me?" but it is also very destructive.

People do not take drugs to punish others in their family. Most often, drugs are a means, however misguided, of helping the user cope with his or her life. Therefore, the family must realize that no amount of pleading or urging will change an addict's behavior. They must also understand that it may be of great help to the addict if they alter theirs.

Drug abusers need more love, understanding, and support. Sadly, this may be the most difficult time for the family to offer these feelings. Many people who live with a drug addict find they must struggle to come to terms with their own attitudes first. Because this is such a difficult thing to do, they often turn to family support groups such as Families Anonymous or Al-Anon. Here family members learn how others have managed to cope with the same problems. They learn how to get on with their own needs and lives despite the problem that has invaded their home. They become familiar with the ground rules for dealing with a drug user.

Among the first things that family members must learn is how to stop helping the addict continue to abuse drugs. The family must stop covering up. They must stop avoiding the truth, and they must stop hiding the problem from one another and from others. Above all, they must confront the user in the family with the consequences of his or her addiction. It is vital that no one protect the addict from the effects that drug use has on everyone else in the house.

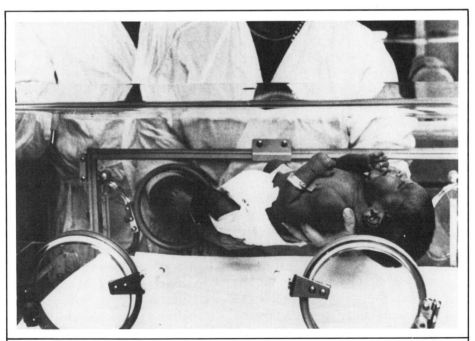

Born to a heroin abuser, this two-day-old infant himself became addicted in the womb. At a hospital in Philadelphia, he suffers the agonies of withdrawal, including hyperactivity, screaming, and irritability.

No one in the family may ever lend a drug user any money. They must become aware of any cash or valuables that may be missing from the house. Nothing of value should be left around to tempt a drug user. Addicts can be desperate and will often do anything to obtain the drug they need. The family cannot be the source of funds for the addict's next fix.

No one in the family may allow drugs to be used while he or she is around. If there is no way to stop the user, the kindest thing to do is just to walk away. It is imperative not to stay in the room and imply any kind of approval, but it is useless to lecture the user, to lose one's temper, argue, moralize, or scold.

The family can best help by becoming informed about available treatment for drug users and their families. They can encourage the user to contact a source of help. There are many organizations that will assist the family by supplying the information they may need.

The family does the most harm by telling the user that he or she is no good and not worth helping. The worst possible thing that those who are close to a drug addict can do is to "write off" the user as hopeless and beyond treatment. Ridicule or shame only worsens the problem. The family must firmly believe that there is a good chance for recovery, if not for the addict, then surely for those who live with an addict. They must come to realize that family members, as well as the drug abuser, are victims of addiction and in need of treatment.

Treating the Family

Today experts understand that all persons who live with drug abusers are themselves potential clients for treatment. The concept of offering help to the families of addicts dates back to the founding of Al-Anon in the 1940s. Al-Anon arose as a parallel, but separate, organization to Alcoholics Anonymous. It was designed to help nonalcoholic spouses, children, and close friends of alcoholics deal with the problem of alcoholism. Today Al-Anon continues to help people learn how to recover from the effects of living with an alcoholic and reaches out to families of cocaine and heroin addicts, as well.

Family treatment has become an important part of the programs at many drug rehabilitation centers throughout the

A scene from a TV commercial in which a father confronts his son with a cache of drugs. Honest communication is difficult but necessary in helping a family member come to terms with a substance abuse problem.

country. The Betty Ford Center in California offers one of the finest family programs of its kind. The staff at the center strongly believes that the entire family is caught up in the progression of a user's drug dependency. They offer an intensive 5- to 10-day treatment process for family members and close friends that includes drug education as well as individual and group therapy. The center also conducts special sessions for children between the ages of 6 and 18.

The Children of Addiction

Of all those who come in contact with addiction, the children of alcholics and other addicts pay the highest price. Each year an incredible burden is inherited by the many thousands of children who are born to addicted mothers. In New York City alone there are more than 127,000 women who are known to abuse drugs. Most of these women, like their counterparts all over the country, are part of a continuing cycle of drug dependence, child neglect, and family breakup.

A typical example is that of Cheryl D., a heroin addict and the mother of a 16-month-old son. Cheryl's mother, who herself is recovering from 20 years of drug abuse, saw her own children raised in a series of foster homes. When Cheryl became pregnant, she was told by a social service worker that the child she was carrying might be taken away from her. Cheryl, who well knew the pitfalls of the foster care system, did not want her child to be taken away. Fortunately for her and her son, Cheryl was one of the lucky ones.

Most children of drug abusers are doomed to a life of neglect and deprivation, but Cheryl and her baby found a haven on Ward's Island in New York City. They entered Odyssey House, a unique program that offers a residential treatment program for substance-addicted parents and their children.

Former First Lady Betty Ford leaving the hospital after receiving treatment for alcohol and drug abuse in 1978. She went on to found the Betty Ford Center, a drug treatment facility that has helped thousands of patients overcome their own addictions.

In 1971, Odyssey House opened its doors to men and women age 17 and up with a history of addiction who have children (including newborns) up to age 5. Pregnant or unwed mothers, single parents, and family groups may apply for help. In fact, 1 out of every 15 residents at Odyssey House is a father.

This special treatment facility has a 24-hour open-door policy. Addicted persons with children come here voluntarily or may be referred by their families, friends, hospitals, courts, prisons, or social service agencies. They come for the chance to end their addictions as they learn the skills they will need to become good parents. The program offers individual and group therapy, parenting workshops, and education classes. The "graduates" of Odyssey House leave drug-free and better equipped to meet the needs of their children.

Drug abusers in the program who cannot adequately care for their children may turn to the center for assistance in the form of foster care or adoption. All residents first sign an agreement that allows Odyssey House to arrange for the placement and care of their youngsters if they leave the program before completing treatment. However, many parents and children complete the program and are then prepared to go on with their lives. Some choose to join self-sustaining family cooperatives, where they pool their resources and live together as an extended family.

The concern for children of drug abusers is widening. In New York City, a remarkable woman known as "Mother" Clara Hale has taken thousands of babies into her home. Born to addicted mothers, these infants come into the world with a physiological dependency on whatever drug their mother is abusing. They go through withdrawal under Hale's care and remain in her charge until appropriate homes can be found for them.

The Children of Alcoholics

Alcohol has always led the list of addictive substances that leave terrible scars on the whole family. Today more than 28 million adults and children are living with, or grew up in, households with an alcoholic parent. An alarming number of these children also become alcoholics and continue the cycle of family disruption.

Clara Hale at Hale House, a group foster home she founded in New York City for the infants of addicts. As many as 9,000 children are born addicted to heroin each year in the United States alone.

In *When Your Parent Drinks Too Much*, Eric Ryerson describes how the lives of children of alcoholics are filled with fear, humiliation, and broken promises. Living with an alcoholic parent is a lonely and isolated experience, because most families try to deny the problem and keep it hidden from others. Anger, hurt, and guilt take their toll on these children at very early ages. Their lives are characterized by tension and anxiety, neglect and mistreatment. The children of alcoholics live without consistency and a profound sense of having been abandoned.

Children of alcoholics carry their burden for the rest of their lives. As adults, they have great difficulty leading normal lives and carrying on healthy relationships. Janet Geringer Woititz, president of the Institute for Counseling and Training in Verona, New Jersey, wrote a best-selling book about this problem. In *Adult Children of Alcoholics*, Woititz describes how grown children of alcoholics judge themselves harshly and often develop very low levels of self-esteem. They are both highly self-critical and overly sensitive to the criticism of others.

Many adult children of alcoholics are prone to lying, having long experienced the need to deny and cover up and having been lied to for most of their lives. They have difficulty expressing their real feelings and often cannot separate love from pity. Understandably, they bring these deeply rooted problems into their adult relationships, where they often feel insecure and distrustful.

Fortunately, there are support groups for both young and adult children of alcoholics. Such groups are designed to teach them how to deal with an alcoholic parent and how to get on with their own needs and lives.

Al-Anon and Alateen help family members throughout the country cope with the tragic effects of alcoholism. The National Association for Children of Alcoholics (COA) in Laguna, California, can provide information about local chapters and support groups. ACOA, an organization for Adult Children of Alcoholics, also has many local chapters and a good track record of helping adults work through their problems.

The Drunkard, *an ancient Roman statue. Through the ages, most societies have tolerated the use of alcohol. Perhaps this is why it has been responsible for more suffering and death than any other drug.*

CHAPTER 5

ALCOHOLISM

Alcohol is the cause of more deaths, violence, family disruption, and job absenteeism than any other substance. This legal and readily available drug is regularly consumed by more than 175 million men, women, and young people in the United States alone.

Alcoholism is a major drug-abuse problem that has been overshadowed by the growing concern over marijuana, heroin, and cocaine abuse. Yet alcohol seriously affects one out of every 10 Americans who drink, and as we have said, estimates place the number of alcoholics in the United States today at between 10 and 13 million. These men and women have little or no control over their drinking and need alcohol with the same urgency a heroin addict needs his fix. At the same time, millions of other people are problem drinkers who have taken the first steps on the road toward alcohol addiction.

Alcohol and Its Effects

Alcohol affects different people in different ways. Some people are easily intoxicated, while others have almost no reaction to alcohol. One person may drink a great deal of alcohol and never become addicted, but another person's move toward alcoholism may begin with his or her very first drink. The state of intoxication itself also varies from user to

A homeless man on the streets of New York City. Many of the nation's homeless are the victims of alcoholism or schizophrenia.

user. Some people are loud and extroverted, while others become silent and withdrawn. One person who is drunk may be aggressive and violent, while another is depressed and weepy.

Whatever its form, alcoholism is an extremely serious condition in need of treatment. For many years, society viewed alcoholics as criminals to be fined or imprisoned. For the past two decades, most experts have come to agree that addiction to alcohol is a primary (meaning that it is a disease in itself and not a symptom of some underlying psychological condition), progressive, and potentially fatal disease.

The first steps leading to a greater understanding that alcoholism was a disease were taken by the founders of AA in 1939. Soon after, in the mid-1940s, Dr. E. M. Jellinek formally introduced this belief to the medical community. Dr. Jellinek understood that the more a person drinks, the more alcohol that person needs. He presented the view that alcoholism, as an illness, progresses from moderate to heavier and heavier drinking, and continues until the alcoholic either breaks down or stops drinking. If the drinking stops, the disease is halted, and the person is considered to be recovering, but never cured. Should the alcoholic ever drink again, the disease comes out of its state of remission, and the cycle is renewed.

Ten years later, the American Medical Association officially recognized alcoholism as a disease. This important step allowed alcoholics to seek help for this condition just as they might for any other illness. Also, in 1962, the U.S. Supreme Court ruled that an illness cannot be considered a crime. This paved the way for alcoholism to be legally viewed as a condition to be treated rather than punished. The alcoholic would no longer be thrown into prison or fined as a criminal but would be referred to a treatment program for help.

By 1970 many agencies, both public and private, began to address the problem. At this time, the federal government created the National Institute on Alcohol Abuse and Alcoholism (NIAA). This effort made funds available to the states for planning and establishing research and treatment facilities for alcoholism. As a result, hundreds of treatment centers and clinics around the country now offer hope to people who suffer from drinking problems. Alcohol treatment programs differ from one another in a number of ways, but it is encouraging to note that 35–50% of all alcoholics who do undergo treatment recover completely.

Types of Treatment

There is a variety of techniques for treating alcoholism, the most successful of which, as we have said, incorporate the principles of AA. However, as with any illness, no single treatment works for all patients. It is important to realize that victims of alcoholism do have choices and may find greater relief from one therapy than from another.

Psychotherapy is a treatment for alcoholism that may be offered by a psychiatrist, psychologist, social worker, or alcoholism counselor. Professionals who use this method try to help the alcoholic understand why he or she started drinking in the first place. They believe that the abuse of alcohol often is a way of masking emotions, such as anger, fear, or depression, that the person cannot handle properly.

Behavior modification therapy is another treatment method that, unlike traditional therapy, is not concerned with uncovering the reasons why people drink to excess. Behavior modification focuses on drinking as a learned behavior. It attempts to replace destructive drinking habits with new, more desirable behavior patterns. In order to modify or change these patterns, behavior modification uses systems of reward and punishment to reshape the alcoholic's life-style.

Drug therapy is another alternative open to alcoholics. Some doctors treat drug addiction by administering drugs that produce unpleasant reactions to alcohol. Antabuse, which is a trade name for disulfiram, helps patients resist drinking. After taking this medication for five days, the alcohol user will experience headaches, vomiting, dizziness, double vision, and breathing difficulties if he or she drinks alcohol. Doctors also may prescribe mild tranquilizers or antidepressants to ease withdrawal symptoms. One major problem with drug therapy is the danger of a new dependency. Replacing one drug with another does not end addiction but may successfully stop alcohol consumption.

Hospital treatment programs are offered by hundreds of hospitals across the country. Many of these are modeled after the program at Long Beach Naval Hospital in California, where

A speaker at an Alcoholics Anonymous meeting, where the only requirement for membership is "a desire to stop drinking."

TWELVE STEPS

AWAKENING
CONSCIOUS
CONTINUED
AMENDS
WILLING
HUMBLY
READY
ADMIT
SEARCHING
DECISION
BELIEVE
ADMITTED

TO SOBRIETY

A member of Alcoholics Anonymous drew this representation of the group's 12 Steps, communicating the spirituality that suffuses the program.

Betty Ford and Billy Carter, the brother of former president Jimmy Carter, received treatment. Most hospital programs include a detoxification unit, should it be required for an entering patient. Activities for patients include small therapy groups that stress openness, candor, and sharing. Here alcoholics examine the reasons for their loss of control. The group builds up feelings of trust and support among its members and works to break down the patterns of denial and self-deceit that so often characterize the alcoholic.

Most hospital treatment centers require that patients attend AA meetings every evening. The daily routines for alcoholics during treatment include group lectures, psychodrama sessions, regular work assignments, physical ac-

A patron browsing in a liquor store. For most people, drinking is a harmless practice that enhances sociability. But for 10 to 13 million Americans, it is the agent of a life-threatening addiction.

tivities such as calisthenics and jogging, and maintaining a nutritious diet.

State treatment programs have been established in most states through funds provided by the NIAA. The State of New York Division of Alcoholism and Alcohol Abuse is a fine example of the extensive state services provided to alcoholics and their families. The program operates inpatient facilities in hospitals, alcoholism treatment centers, and alcohol crisis centers. Its outpatient program is carried on at alcoholism clinics and other special centers that help people to readjust their lives after rehabilitation.

The New York State programs stress that recovery from alcoholism begins with abstinence but must continue to focus on the need to make significant social and psychological changes. The program recognizes the role that spiritual experiences play in bringing about these changes. As a result, they strongly encourage their clients to become involved in AA, which, as we will see later in the chapter, stresses spiritual awakening.

The New York State program is based on three major steps. The first of these is withdrawal. Some patients need a structured experience in dealing with this problem and may be sent to an alcohol crisis center for help. Most withdrawal treatment, however, is done on an outpatient basis.

The second step is aimed at stabilizing the patient. During this phase, the alcoholic must confront the psychological effects of his or her drinking. Counseling as well as individual and group therapy helps alcoholics to circumvent their psychological dependence and to break down their defense systems. At this stage there is a great emphasis on the prevention of possible relapses.

Finally, the program deals with rehabilitation. Patients are helped to reorder and restructure their lives to make it possible for them to survive in a nonalcoholic world. There is much focus on the spiritual growth of the recovering alcoholic so that he or she may develop a sense of well-being, happiness, and purpose.

The programs in New York State embrace a holistic approach to rehabilitation — they believe that health is a state of balance between the mind and the body. As a result, they employ a variety of methods such as meditation, acupuncture, self-hypnosis, visual imagery, and biofeedback to help alcoholics grow emotionally, socially, and spiritually. They also operate an Employment Program for Recovering Alcoholics (EPRA). This service, which is a vital part of the recovery program, helps alcoholics speed their recovery by attaining gainful employment.

Women for Sobriety (WFS) was organized in 1976 as a self-help program for women alcoholics. The first national organization of its kind, WFS now has hundreds of groups in the United States and abroad that attempt to deal with what they consider to be the special needs of alcoholic women. The groups, which meet in private homes, offer women an alternative to the program of AA.

WFS was founded by Jean Kirkpatrick, a two-time dropout from AA. Once it became obvious that the AA recovery rate was significantly higher for males than for females, Kirkpatrick became convinced that women needed a different program. Her conviction that the emotional needs of women in alcohol recovery are very different from males led to the formation of a 13-step philosophy that WFS calls the "New Life" program.

Kirkpatrick points out that men drink in public places, whereas women generally drink in private. "Men drink for a sense of power, while women drink out of frustration, helplessness, and dependency," says Kirkpatrick, who also is concerned that 9 out of 10 wives remain with recovering husbands, but only 1 out of 10 husbands remains with a recovering wife. Kirkpatrick feels that many of the five million women alcoholics in the United States lack positive feelings about themselves. They have little or no self-respect and surrender what is left to alcohol.

The "New Life" Program of WFS encourages positive thinking and self-esteem. The ideology of the program can be summed up as "I am what I think." Each of the 13 statements in the program encourages women to take charge of their own bodies and thoughts. "I am a competent woman, and have much to give to life," WFS members assert. The emphasis is on learning to cope with life and becoming independent. The goal is to put the past behind and to find ego strengths that will ensure the future.

In contrast to the AA philosophy, WFS rejects the need to learn humility. Jean Kirkpatrick claims that humility is the last thing a woman needs. What she needs, say the women of WFS, is a good self-image and a strong ego. WFS hopes to help women change their way of life by first changing their way of thinking.

Alcoholics Anonymous (AA)

Without any doubt, the organization with the best track record for promoting recovery from alcoholism is AA. Co-founded by Bill Wilson and Dr. Robert Smith in 1939, AA remains the inspiration for hundreds of alcohol self-help and treatment programs all over the world.

Today there are more than 50,000 AA groups meeting in more than 110 different countries. Wherever its more than 2 million members meet, whatever the language they speak, the core of the AA Fellowship, as members call themselves, remains the same: "Each day, somewhere in the world, recovery begins when one alcoholic talks with another alcoholic, sharing experience, strength, and hope."

AA is an organization that helps alcoholics help themselves and each other to sober up and stay sober. At AA

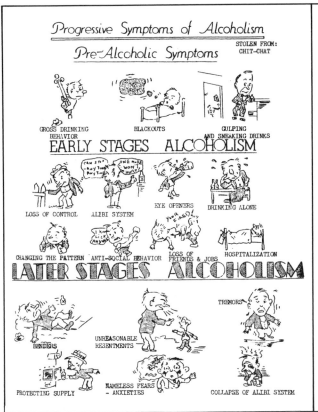

Progressive Symptoms of Alcoholism

Pre-Alcoholic Symptoms

This series of cartoons, depicting the various warning signs and symptoms of alcoholism through its progressive stages, was drawn by a member of Alcoholics Anonymous.

meetings, members share their experiences with alcoholism. Recovering alcoholics tell how they were able to free themselves of alcohol dependence. Members offer one another advice, support, and comfort. Their mutual goal is not to be cured of alcoholism but to abstain from drinking "one day at a time."

The AA program is based on spiritual principles. It leads its members to a spiritual awakening, a transformation that relieves the craving for alcohol and brings about inner comfort and a significant change in personality. AA has no formal religious affiliation and asks only that its members submit to a "higher power" as each understands it.

The sole purpose of the AA program is to promote the sobriety of is members. The program of recovery is based on Twelve Steps and Twelve Traditions that guide its membership.

The Twelve Steps of Alcoholics Anonymous

1. We admitted we were powerless over alcohol and that our lives had become unmanageable.
2. We came to believe that a Power greater than ourselves could restore us to sanity.
3. We made a decision to turn our will and our lives over to the care of God as we understood Him.
4. We made a searching and fearless moral inventory of ourselves.
5. We admitted to God, to ourselves, and to another human being the exact nature of our wrongs.
6. We were entirely ready to have God remove all these defects of character.
7. We humbly asked Him to remove our shortcomings.
8. We made a list of all persons we had harmed, and became willing to make amends to them all.
9. We made direct amends to such people wherever possible, except when to do so would injure them or others.
10. We continued to take personal inventory and when we were wrong promptly admitted it.
11. We sought through prayer and meditation to improve our conscious contact with God as we understood Him, praying only for knowledge of His will for us and the power to carry that out.
12. Having had a spiritual awakening as the result of these steps, we tried to carry this message to alcoholics and to practice these principles in all our affairs.

The Twelve Traditions of Alcoholics Anonymous

1. Our common welfare should come first; personal recovery depends upon AA unity.
2. For our group purpose there is but one ultimate authority — a loving God as He may express Himself in our group conscience. Our leaders are but trusted servants; they do not govern.
3. The only requirement for AA membership is a desire to stop drinking.

4. Each group should be autonomous except in matters affecting other groups or AA as a whole.
5. Each group has but one primary purpose — to carry its message to the alcoholic who still suffers.
6. An AA group ought never endorse, finance, or lend the AA name to any related facility or outside enterprise, lest problems of money, property, and prestige divert us from our primary purpose.
7. Every AA group ought to be fully self-supporting, declining outside contributions.
8. AA should remain forever nonprofessional, but our service centers may employ special workers.
9. AA, as such, ought never to be organized; but we may create service boards or committees directly responsible to those they serve.
10. AA has no opinion on outside issues; hence the AA name ought never be drawn into public controversy.
11. Our public relations policy is based on attraction rather than promotion; we need always maintain personal anonymity at the level of press, radio, and films.
12. Anonymity is the spiritual foundation of all our traditions, ever reminding us to place principles before personalities.

By faithfully adhering to its Steps and Traditions, Alcoholics Anonymous has been the hope and haven of millions of people who are addicted to alcohol and other drugs. The AA program is an integral part of the treatment used by other clinics and hospitals throughout the country and continues to offer parallel support services for the friends, spouses, and children of addicts, as well.

The recovering member of AA accepts the fact that he or she will always be an alcoholic. There is no shame, no regret, only pride in a newly found strength and fellowship. Millions of anonymous recovering alcoholics as well as noted AA members such as Daniel J. Travanti, Robert Young, and Dick Van Dyke are a testimony to the fact that for those who are willing and able to commit themselves to its methods, the AA program works.

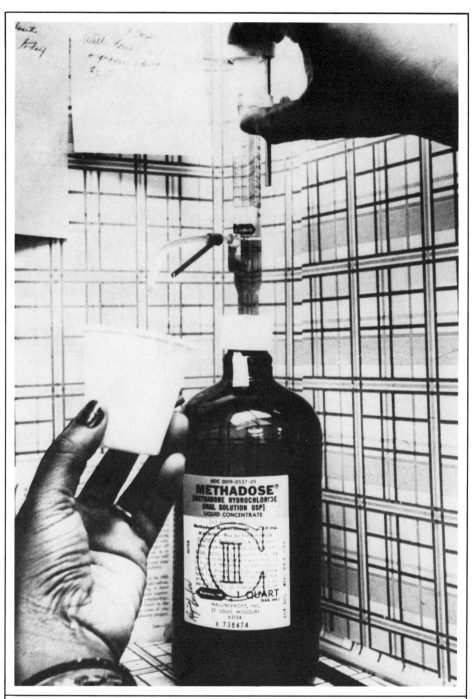

Methadone is dispensed in liquid form in measured doses. Methadone maintenance is the standard form of treatment for heroin addiction.

CHAPTER 6

METHADONE MAINTENANCE

During the 1980s, the problem of heroin addiction has taken a backseat to a greater concern about abuse of cocaine and crack. Throughout the century, heroin has been the drug of choice among rather limited groups of users. For a long time it was popular among musicians and entertainers, and eventually it found its way into the "hippie" subculture that flourished in the 1960s. As the heroin market increased, its most vulnerable victims became members of inner-city minorities. Only when heroin-related crime spilled violently into the streets of middle America was the public at large moved to call for action.

A heroin addict needs a fix every four or five hours. By the time an addiction is firmly established in the user's system, the heroin addict often is more concerned with avoiding withdrawal than with getting a "high." The desperation for relief results in a heroin habit that may easily cost hundreds of dollars a day to maintain. To pay for their drugs, most users resort to dealing drugs, to prostitution, and to stealing.

Treating the heroin addict is no easy task. Detoxification programs and self-help groups such as Synanon have found that only about 1 in 10 heroin users remains drug-free for more than two years after leaving a treatment program. Since methadone maintenance was introduced in the mid-1960s, this approach has become the standard, most widely financed form of treatment for heroin addiction in the United States.

Dr. Vincent Dole (left) with his son and the late Robert Kennedy at a New York State Senate hearing on narcotics addiction in 1965. During the early 1960s, Dole and Dr. Marie Nyswander conducted the first experiments in methadone maintenance.

The Methadone Program

Methadone was first developed as an analgesic (pain remover) by the Germans during World War II. After the war, it was studied by a sub-committee of the U.S. State Department and marketed here under the names Dolphine, Adinon, Amidonem, and Althose.

As early as 1948, methadone was used to detoxify heroin addicts. Then, in the early 1960s, the drug's potential use as a means to counteract heroin abuse was discovered accidentally at Rockefeller University. At this time, Dr. Vincent Dole, a specialist in biochemistry, was doing extensive research on metabolic diseases, diseases that are caused by chemical changes in the cells of the body. In 1963, Dr. Dole joined forces with Dr. Marie Nyswander, a noted psychiatrist, who had a great deal of experience working with drug addicts.

The two doctors teamed up to try to find a way to relieve the craving for drugs. Their research led to the discovery that methadone, a synthetic, or artificial, narcotic, could suc-

cessfully block the effects of heroin in the body. With Dr.
Nyswander, Dr. Dole carried on the first experiments in methadone maintenance ever attempted.

Drs. Dole and Nyswander began their methadone program in 1965 with only six heroin addicts. Less than a decade later, almost 70,000 addicts were being maintained in more than 450 programs all over the country.

The major goal of methadone maintenance programs is to help patients learn to function effectively in their daily lives, once their dependency on heroin has been overcome. After an addict is admitted to the program, he or she is expected to remain free from criminal activity. He or she is also expected to find and hold a job and cease his or her consumption of heroin and all other drugs, as well. The key to the program, of course, is that the addict receives a daily dose of methadone, the drug that can relieve the user of all craving for heroin.

No single dosage of methadone blocks the effect of heroin in all addicts. The entering patient receives greater and greater amounts of the drug until a stabilization dose is reached. This is the amount that is effective for any individual heroin addict and may vary from 30 to 120 milligrams a day. Because the blocking effect of methadone lasts for only 24 hours, the addict must appear at the maintenance center faithfully for a new dose of medication.

The methadone patient must take the drug by mouth. If methadone is taken by injection, it produces a narcotic "high." As a result, it normally is administered at the maintenance clinics in the form of a tablet or a liquid that resembles a soft drink. At first, patients must come each day for their dose of methadone. When they arrive, they have their urine tested to determine that they have taken no other drugs. The patients are watched very carefully and must take the drug in the presence of a worker at the center.

As addicts show they can be trusted, they often are permitted to come in every other day. Some clinics even allow some patients to take home an entire week's supply of methadone. If taken in the form of a soft drink, methadone must be transported and refrigerated in a locked box. This is done so that it is not mistaken for orange juice or another harmless drink. Most clinics prefer to administer methadone tablets, which do not require refrigeration and are less likely to fall into the hands of unsuspecting children.

However often the addict appears at the clinic, the commitment to treatment must last a lifetime. To remain free from the craving for heroin and the effects of withdrawal, the patient must continue to take methadone as long as he or she lives. As it turns out, this is not a difficult thing to do, as methadone is as addictive a drug as heroin.

Even though it is a narcotic, methadone, when taken orally, does not supply the euphoria, or feeling of well-being, experienced from heroin use. The patient remains alert and energetic, has no withdrawal symptoms, and can function as well as a nonaddict.

There are some mild side effects from methadone use. Some patients experience weight gain, constipation, excessive perspiration, nausea, or insomnia. However, any inconveniences are balanced by the low cost of maintaining a methadone habit. In contrast to the hundreds of dollars needed for heroin, methadone maintenance costs about five dollars per person per day.

The Problems

Methadone maintenance has been successful in achieving its primary goals. It serves as an effective response to the public's demand for immediate action against heroin-related crime. It is a method that offers heroin addicts almost immediate relief from their craving for an illegal drug. It places addicts in the hands of doctors and clinics instead of judges and prisons. And, to some, the best things about maintenance is that it results not only in reduced crime but in lower law enforcement, penal, and welfare expenditures, as well. In short, it saves the public money.

In spite of this success, methadone maintenance has long been the target of a great deal of criticism and controversy. It has been called a "technological fix," which serves the needs of society rather than the needs of the heroin addict. It is viewed by many people as a simple pharmacological solution for a complicated social, political, and psychological problem.

In fact, few maintenance programs offer heroin addicts anything other than a way to transfer their craving to a less debilitating drug. Most methadone programs located in large cities service thousands of addicts. There are long waiting lists for acceptance into the clinics as well as long lines of addicts to be treated daily. The typical treatment generally is limited to the distribution of methadone and offers the addict no psychotherapy, vocational rehabilitation, or group support.

Those in charge of methadone maintenance are well aware that many serious problems confront the program. They acknowledge that 25% of methadone users also abuse alcohol. In any one year, there are more deaths from the combined use of methadone and alcohol (or another drug) than from overdosing on heroin itself. Some patients in methadone treatment, in a misguided attempt to treat themselves or to make money off the excess, take only a part of the dosage required to keep them heroin-free. Since low doses reduce but do not eliminate the craving for heroin, many methadone patients continue to use heroin.

In many cases, the methadone program does not fully determine the extent of a potential patient's addiction. A

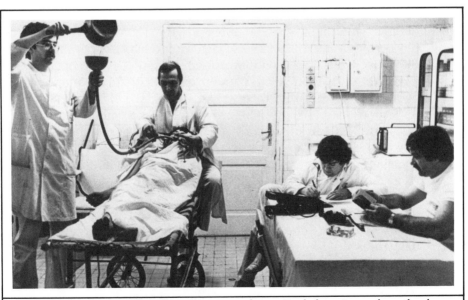

Doctors treat a victim of a drug overdose. Both heroin and methadone overdoses can lead to unconsciousness and even death.

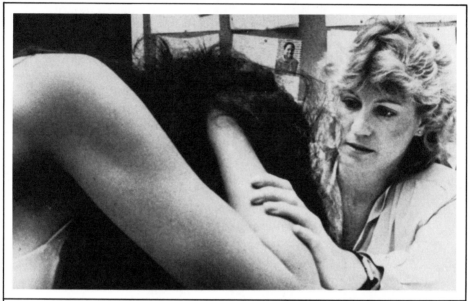

A counselor at a California clinic comforts a runaway who resorted to prostitution to support her drug habit. Methadone maintenance frees addicts from their desperate and often violent search for drug money.

number of heroin users who enter programs are not actually physically addicted. They are, in fact, turned into addicts after they have been placed on methadone. Also, there have been a number of cases in which patients have died of methadone overdoses at the clinics themselves.

Another serious problem is street trafficked methadone. Many addicts use methadone to bring their heroin habits down to a less expensive level. Methadone, or "dolly" as it is called in street terms, is hard to make and obtain illegally. As a result, most of the illegal supply comes from patients in methadone programs. It is not uncommon for a drug dealer to enter a program disguised as an addict in order to get hold of a methadone supply. Street methadone is an extremely dangerous drug because the same dose of it that an addict can tolerate can prove lethal to a nonaddict. The extent of the problem was highlighted by a January, 1972, *New York Times* survey of clinics in 14 major cities. The survey showed that every one of the clinics had found evidence of extensive methadone trafficking.

In many cities, private physicians also may administer methadone to heroin addicts. In one case, a single physician was discovered to have treated 15,000 heroin users without any adequate evidence that any of them was really addicted. It is logical to assume that a good deal of the methadone that is obtained by loose prescription practices winds up on the illicit drug market.

To further complicate the situation, many addicts on methadone maintenance face serious problems that are rooted in the nature of the program itself. Often, they find it difficult to adjust to the rigid 24-hour routine that the program demands. Adapting to a tightly structured, rule-bound regimen that is radically different from the addict's past life is beyond the psychological resources of many methadone patients. Now that he or she does not have to hustle on the street, the addict is faced with the problem of what to do with this new freedom and spare time. Boredom and isolation often come to characterize the methadone user's life.

Much of the methadone patient's isolation comes from being rejected by both nonaddicts and former addicts alike. To non-addicts, the methadone user is still an addict. To former addicts who were able to break their habits and become drug-free, the methadone addict is viewed as a junkie who does not have the courage to face withdrawal and make a clean break from addiction.

Without support systems to help them adjust, many methadone users also find it difficult to find and hold jobs. Without the services that might help them to stabilize their disrupted family and other personal relationships, many methadone maintenance patients are as separated from the mainstream as they were as heroin addicts. They do not experience the conditions necessary for any individual to find and hold a purposeful position in society at large.

The Opposition

At its inception, methadone maintenance was regarded as a major breakthrough in the treatment of drug addiction. Over the years, however, there has been a steadily increasing opposition to its operation. That opposition has come from political, medical, and social leaders. It strongly expresses the

A patient at a New York City hospital takes her daily dose of methadone. Once discharged, she and others like her must show up at methadone clinics on a regular basis to maintain the proper dosage of the drug.

concerns of people who are convinced that, in the long run, methadone maintenance does not work. Many people who are critical of the program point out that heroin and cocaine once were mistakenly regarded as substances that could be used to cure opium addiction. They say that methadone maintenance does not confront any of the social or psychological problems that lead people to addiction. They feel that over a period of time methadone alone cannot offer an addict the satisfactions that heroin used to supply.

Daniel Casriel, the psychiatric superintendent at Daytop Village in New York City, a residental treatment center, has called the methadone program "malpractice, and a cop-out . . . a cheap substitute for an expensive habit of self-indulgence." Casriel feels that government agencies increase and encourage drug use when they give out free drugs of any kind. He agrees with other critics who say that maintenance does not confront or erase the problems of the heroin addict.

Heroin addiction is primarily an inner-city problem, and its victims are primarily the poor and unemployed. Because of this, politicians such as New York City congressman Charles B. Rangel are opposed to methadone maintenance because they see it as a superficial therapy being imposed on blacks and other minorities who lack the political clout to demand better. Congressman Rangel calls the program a "cheap solution to deal with problems of the poor." He believes that the program would be far different if heroin addiction had spread more extensively into more affluent groups in society.

Political involvement in methadone maintenance also stems from the competition for government funding for treatment programs. Other drug-abuse programs feel that they cannot get a fair share of available funds because the methadone program is the least expensive one to operate and hence most attractive to bureaucrats with the power of purse. Representatives of a number of therapeutic community programs feel that this lack of financial support has denied the heroin addict any real choice of treatment methods.

One such community program is DEN, a New York City drug abstention program whose letters stand for Direction and Education of Narcotics. DEN is an inner-city, street-level organization that has not been successful in securing government money for its program. Its members go out into the community to identify drug users and to bring them into their detoxification programs.

The DEN philosophy is that the addict must be helped to "live life and not just give up drugs." To this end, the program provides its members with regular follow-up and counseling services. Former addicts who have been helped by the DEN program often return to DEN-sponsored parties and social events to help in the rehabilitation of new members. In this way, drug addicts have a new "family" to support their efforts to become drug-free. DEN members, unlike marginal, isolated methadone users, are helped to return to the community.

Additional opposition to unlimited methadone maintenance comes from the medical community. In December 1985, John J. McCarthy, M.D., and Orin T. Borders, Ph.D., wrote of their concern in the *American Journal of Psychia-*

Proponents of methadone maintenance argue that even if it replaces one addiction with another, it at least helps protect the addict population from some of the ravages of intravenous drug use.

try. Their article stated that the effectiveness of methadone maintenance has greatly diminished since its early successes. The doctors document "chronic drug abuse and continued drug dealing around clinics by many patients receiving methadone." They trace part of the problem to the fact that the methadone maintenance population is becoming younger and more psychologically disturbed than it had been and more prone to abuse more than one drug. McCarthy and Borders also find that the effectiveness of methadone maintenance has been undermined by changes that have been made in the program over the past 16 years. The original program was more structured than those in operation today. Originally, clinics conducted frequent urine tests and dismissed patients for alcohol or other drug abuse. Patients also could be dismissed or placed on probation if they displayed behavior problems. Today, because of lax supervision, such measures are no longer taken at most clinics.

McCarthy and Borders conducted a study at a University of California methadone program. They found that when patients know they will be withdrawn from a program for drug use, they voluntarily decrease or end their involvement with drugs. They also tend to remain in treatment programs for longer periods of time.

It seems, then, that methadone maintenance has not lived up to the hopes that were held out for it in the late 1960s. To be sure, there are addicts for whom methadone is the only practical way to escape the craving for heroin. And there are methadone centers that are able to provide therapeutic, educational, and employment programs for their patients. However, the opposition to methadone is becoming more outspoken.

Methadone maintenance programs have to take a closer look at their long-term effects. They will have to consider the criticism that they offer little more than a drug-oriented "tranquilizing" approach to a very complex problem.

Already, many clinics are encouraging gradual detoxification — over the course of a year in some cases — rather than the traditional maintenance. However, if methadone is to be used at all in the treatment of heroin addiction, it seems that it will have to be as an adjunct to therapies that address the needs and difficulties of the individual as a whole.

First Lady Nancy Reagan embraces a resident of Daytop Village after the drug rehabilitation center presented her with its Promethean Award. Mrs. Reagan has spearheaded a national campaign against drug abuse.

CHAPTER 7

A LOOK AT TREATMENT CENTERS

The need for treatment facilities has been recognized by every community that has felt the consequences of drug abuse. Thousands of treatment centers have been established throughout the United States. Some are free of charge to anyone who seeks help at their doors; others are within the reach only of those addicts who can pay thousands of dollars for treatment.

Unfortunately, there are many more people in need of treatment than there are places equipped to help them. Throughout the country, hospitals, clinics, and therapeutic communities are forced to turn away hundreds of addicts each day for lack of room. Some addicts must travel far to receive help, whereas others are placed on long waiting lists.

Anyone with a substance-abuse problem must be helped to understand that it is impossible to conquer an addiction alone. He or she must also be assured that with the right treatment it is possible to become and remain drug-free.

With that goal in mind, this chapter will take a closer view at some major drug treatment centers. Keep in mind that alcoholism and drug abuse go hand in hand. Few centers today treat one kind of addiction to the exclusion of all others. We have already discussed some programs that emphasize a particular addiction, or focus on a special category of clients.

Now we will examine more closely several drug treatment programs that have met with significant success. This does not mean that everyone who enters the program is guaranteed a drug-free exit. It does not mean that those who kick their habit will never return to it. It does mean, however, that large numbers of people have found a place to give them a new lease on life and to help them do what they thought could never be done — namely, learn to live without drugs. It also proves that drug addiction does not have to be a lifelong affliction.

The Betty Ford Center

Barnaby Conrad, a noted writer and artist, spent 30 years denying that he was an alcoholic. At the age of 63, he checked into the Betty Ford Center for 30 days of treatment. During this time, he was able to gain control of the addiction that had nearly destroyed his life. In *Time Is All We Have*, a candid account of his treatment experience, Conrad describes his first view of the Betty Ford Center in Rancho Mirage, California:

> Floating there in the desert in a sea of grass, newly cut, was what appeared to be a country club ... It looked like an elegant clubhouse ... and off to the left was a large pond with three swans gliding gracefully on it.

The Betty Ford Center is purposely designed to look nothing like an institution. Located in a beautiful desert setting on the campus of the Eisenhower Medical Center, its four 20-bed residential units might easily be mistaken for comfortable hotel accommodations.

Patients who come to the center are assigned to one of these units. Here all aspects of their treatment, with the exception of meals and lectures, are carried out. The 20 people assigned to each unit become an extended family, providing one another with support and fellowship. They share meals, therapy sessions, and social activities as well as their inner pains and joys.

The Betty Ford Center is well-known for some of its celebrity clients. Liza Minelli, Elizabeth Taylor, Tony Curtis, and Robert Mitchum are among a number of the center's

Liza Minnelli and her manager (now husband) Marc Gero at a New York club in 1978. She is one of many celebrities who overcame addiction to drugs and alcohol through treatment provided at the Betty Ford Center.

most notable graduates. However, while in treatment, these glamorous performers were treated exactly the same as the other men and women, 18 years of age or older, who are regularly welcomed to the center.

The Betty Ford Center lists two toll-free numbers to make it easy to ask for help from anywhere in the world. In California, the number is 800-392-7540. The out-of-state number is 800-854-0033. Normally, there is a waiting list of several hundred potential patients, but the center does whatever it can to place people in its program. The cost for treatment may run as high as the $6,000 that Barnaby Conrad paid for his four-week stay. However, many insurance carriers, such as Blue Cross/Blue Shield, now cover the cost of chemical dependence treatment.

The staff at the center includes physicians, nurses, chemical-dependence counselors, clergy counselors, clinical psychologists, and other health care professionals. It is not uncommon to discover that many staff members are themselves recovering alcoholics or drug addicts.

Betty Ford, who helped found the center after her own bout with alcohol and drugs, plays an active role in the treatment program. She is at the center regularly and speaks to all new patients about her own experience. Mrs. Ford introduces herself at the group lectures with the words "Hello, my name is Betty Ford, and I'm an alcoholic and an addict."

The heart of the treatment program is based on the Twelve Steps of AA. As the patients progress through treatment, they learn to become responsible for their own actions and recovery. They agree not to leave the premises for the duration of their stay and are permitted visitors only after they have been in treatment for a full week, and then only for several hours on Sundays and holidays. Patients may read a newspaper in the evening but are not permitted books or magazines, which are considered to be distracting to their treatment.

A typical day at the Betty Ford Center begins with a "meditation walk" before breakfast. After breakfast, the patient attends to his or her therapeutic duty assignment, taking care of some chore related to daily living. This is followed by a lecture, group therapy sessions, and a lunch. Another lecture and another group therapy session follow lunch.

Later afternoon activities include attending a community meeting with all of the residents and participating in recreational activities, such as swimming or jogging. Study time and quiet time precede supper. After supper there is another lecture and an AA meeting.

Each day's program is designed to provide patients with the tools and principles they need if they hope to go on to a drug-free life. If they remain open and willing, most people in the program have a good chance to achieve this end. However, the program at the Betty Ford Center also recognizes the importance of family treatment. Family members and "significant others" are required to participate in a five-day intensive process of education and therapy. A special children's program, directed at children of alcoholics between the ages of eight and 18, gives young people an opportunity to begin their own recovery with expert help.

The center also offers a number of additional services. It is presently addressing the special needs of women addicts in its women's program. It runs a highly structured and intensive 12-month outpatient program and develops an individual aftercare plan for each patient who is ready to leave treatment. All patients are required to participate in AA, or other similar self-help groups as part of the after-care regimen.

There are many factors that contribute to the success of the Betty Ford Center. Among these is the fact that the center, in its own words, is "a special place, a special staff, loving and caring, and the beginning of acceptance by patients of themselves and their disease."

Phoenix House

Each year thousands of men, women, and children in New York and California turn to Phoenix House for help with all kinds of drug problems. Phoenix House is one of the largest multiservice drug-abuse agencies in the United States. Founded in 1967, Phoenix House now operates a number of dynamic residential, outpatient, prevention, and intervention programs for all forms of drug abuse.

Phoenix House Foundation, which runs all the programs, is a nonprofit organization supported by government funds, foundation grants, and private donations. Patients who enter the programs are charged fees that are based on family income, but no one in need of Phoenix's services is denied admission because of an inability to pay.

People in need of help come to Phoenix House through a number of different channels. Some simply come in off the streets, but most are referred by social workers or counselors or brought in by concerned family members or friends. More and more youngsters are being sent to Phoenix House by schools in which Phoenix drug education and prevention teams have worked.

The Phoenix House Admissions Unit has the responsibility of discovering the best way to help the drug-troubled youths and adults who turn to them for help. The unit screens and evaluates potential patients through a series of interviews.

Of those interviewed, about half are admitted to Phoenix programs, and the rest are referred to other agencies in the community.

More than a third of those who are screened for admission enter residential treatment. These new residents are first assigned to a separate induction facility where they learn about the limits and the rewards of life at a Phoenix House residential center. They are given a picture of life in a close-knit, familylike treatment setting and are led to understand that all residents are expected to behave in a responsible way. They are also told that the cardinal rules that govern life at Phoenix House are absolutely no violence and absolutely no drugs.

The philosophy behind the Phoenix House residential program is based on hard work, responsible behavior, a clean break with the past, and fellowship in a caring, familylike community. Residential treatment is provided at six Phoenix House centers in the New York City area and at Phoenix House/Orange County in Santa Ana, California.

The treatment community provides the resident with comfortable surroundings, companionship, and recreational and cultural activities. It offers an opportunity for drug users to let go of old, negative patterns of behavior and to adopt new, positive ones. The residential centers also give the patient a chance to learn and grow and to complete his education and prepare for a new career.

In return for having so many of their needs met, residents at a treatment center must learn to open up to others, to be honest and caring, and to show a real concern for fellow members in the program. Direction for this change comes from staff members, many of whom are themselves former drug abusers. The Phoenix House staff acts both as counselors and role models for the residents. They demonstrate the attitudes and behavior that the program hopes to instill.

At the heart of the treatment program is the encounter — an intense and highly emotional group session — that tries to cut through, and clear away, much of the emotional debris that stands in the way of mature, responsible behavior. In these probing, sometimes volatile encounters, residents slowly learn the meaning of trust. They gradually come to understand that it is safe to reveal their emotions or other hidden aspects of their lives. When they feel the real concern of their new family and reach out with concerns of their own, residents are ready to gain insights into their own lives and into the lives of others. The encounter experience helps residents in treatment to develop the ability to help themselves and, in turn, to help others.

A very special residential high school is operated by Phoenix House: John F. Kennedy High School, which is located on a 140-acre campus in Westchester County, New York. The school has been designed for young former drug abusers who missed out on their education while they were too involved with drugs to function at school.

At this unique school, youngsters are given opportunities to review and be tutored in many subjects they missed while they were on drugs. Although the program is governed by strict Phoenix House rules of behavior, students are given a curriculum that has been enriched with electives, independent study courses, and chances to earn work-study credits. Catching up on education is the primary reason for residency at the school, and graduation is the real "high."

Another program involves a collaboration of Phoenix House and the New York City Board of Education. The Step One Day School, located in the heart of the city, is open to youngsters whose drug problems have disrupted their education. At Step One, licensed specialized teachers and Phoenix House counselors team up to provide basic, remedial, and secondary education coupled with drug abuse treatment.

This alternative school recognizes the special needs of each student, but does not tolerate drug use or violent behavior. Participation by family members is an important part of the Step One program, which hopes to improve the youngster's home situation and to raise his grades so that he or she may once again function in the public school system.

Phoenix House also operates several outpatient services. The Phoenix Evening Program offers men, women, and young adult drug abusers individual treatment plans that do not require residence in a treatment community. These drug users often are the pillars of middle-class community life — the businessmen, housewives, teachers, lawyers, and other mainstream types who increasingly are involved in drugs. The evening program provides specialized therapy groups, couple or family counseling, and may include referral for individual psychotherapy. A key part of this program is the involvement of an abuser's family members and "significant others" in regular group and counseling sessions.

IMPACT (Intervention Moves Parents and Children Together) is a Phoenix House program designed to utilize peer and parental pressure to change the behavior of adolescents who are still in the early stages of drug abuse. Teenagers may be referred to IMPACT by the admissions unit at Pheonix House. Here they meet in peer therapy groups at least three times a week and share the troubled feelings with which so many young people must struggle. The program offers young people a place to work out their problems and gives them positive alternatives to using drugs.

Parents taking part in IMPACT participate in six weekly educational seminars. During these informational sessions, parents learn about drugs and parenting. Family therapists then see entire families to deal with specific family problems. In these ways, IMPACT helps family members work together to solve their own problems. The IMPACT program continues even after drug use stops and acts as a support for families that need new ways to open channels of communication and to set definite limits against drugs.

Phoenix House has helped thousands of young men and women to conquer drug addiction. In the words of its president, Dr. Mitchell S. Rosenthal, Phoenix House has " . . . seen one [individual] after another reclaim dignity and pride after living the most degrading and self-destructive lives."

Daytop Village

In 1963, Monsignor William B. O'Brien founded Daytop Village, the first drug-free residential treatment program in the eastern United States to use the therapeutic community concept of rehabilitation. Today Daytop operates eight outreach centers and five therapeutic communities across New York State and has international centers in many European countries and the Philippines.

Daytop is a demanding drug program based on the principles of self-help. Its method is to place people with drug problems into tightly controlled environments where, with the help of positive peer pressure, they can learn to face their

Monsignor William B. O'Brien, the founder of Daytop Village. Daytop is a demanding drug program based on the principle of self-help.

inner conflicts without self-deception. The program, which provides a wide range of services for people who have drug problems, is among the most successful in the country. At present, hundreds of candidates are on waiting lists for admission to Daytop facilities.

In its residential program, Daytop Village treats individuals over the age of 13 who have severe drug abuse or addiction problems. These people may be referred by a court, school, hospital, community agency, their family, or friends. After extensive physical and psychological testing, the drug abuser may be accepted for upstate treatment.

The upstate residential therapeutic community offers the patient a highly structured, nurturing environment that is totally drug-free. He or she will be exposed to 24-hour treatment services. A personalized treatment plan will combine individual, group, and family therapy as well as therapeutic workshops that best suit each patient.

While in residence, patients are given educational and vocational help and have access to a wide range of support services. All of these activities and services help the resident to develop healthy relationships, positive values, and a manner that is completely free of drugs.

In order to prepare people for reentry into society, residential programs help them establish positive relationships outside the program while working or going to school. Once he or she is ready, the resident moves out into the community but continues to meet with support groups as an outpatient. If all phases of treatment are completed successfully, the treatment-center staff may recommend "graduation" from the program. A graduate of a Daytop Residential Center is someone who is ready to become a contributing member of his or her community.

Daytop uses both professional and non- or paraprofessional staff to operate its programs. The members of its nonprofessional staff are graduates of the Daytop program who

Daytop Village headquarters in New York City. Daytop operates eight outreach centers and five therapeutic communities across New York State. It also operates centers in Europe and the Philippines.

act as role models for people in treatment, serving as the most effective evidence that drug addiction can be conquered.

Recognizing that many adolescents who use drugs are not yet into serious abuse, the Daytop Outreach Centers are designed to work with youngsters between the ages of 13 and 19 who have moderate drug problems. These community-based programs, attended by troubled young people for approximately 18 months, are divided into two phases.

Daycare, the first phase, is concerned with providing in-depth psychological assistance. Its goal is to create the stability needed to be drug-free and to strengthen family relationships. Each day members in the outreach program receive individual counseling from their own counselor and attend group therapy sessions. The teenagers in treatment attend school taught by Board of Education-certified teachers. They must maintain academic performance so that they can make an easy transition back to their community schools when treatment is completed.

Members also participate in cultural and recreational activities organized by the center. They help with the chores that are part of the daily maintenance of this "second home." They develop a sense of their own center and its surrounding community. These activities, and all other parts of the Daytop outreach program, continue to stress the self-help approach to rehabilitation. Daytop believes in "man helping man to help himself."

Aftercare, phase two of the program, is designed to help members develop their social skills and pursue their educational and vocational goals. During this phase, teenagers in outreach programs return to their schools, attend local colleges, or find jobs. At the same time, they continue to attend group therapy sessions at the center. To help them succeed in their home communities and at outside jobs, the Daytop program offers members several supportive services in the forms of workshops, counseling, therapy, and special-interest groups.

An important part of the outreach program involves parent participation. Parent groups, conducted by trained consultants, provide a support system for parents with troubled children. In their groups, parents learn how to deal with the

Participants in Seed, a drug treatment program in Florida. This program, geared toward young people between the ages of 9 and 17, is controversial because of the extreme peer pressure it encourages.

problems that contribute to family conflict. They learn more about parenting and discover that they are an essential part of their youngster's treatment process. Daytop has a family association that provides treatment services for the families of substance abusers. This may explain why Daytop often is called a "family repair station."

Daytop Village programs have treated tens of thousands of drug abusers. Ninety-two percent of their graduates live drug-free lives. Like Phoenix House, Daytop is supported by state and private funds. Its fees are based on the ability to pay, and no one is turned away for lack of money. A 24-hour, toll-free hot line, 1-800-2-DAYTOP, is available to those in the New York area who need help.

The Betty Ford Center, Phoenix House, and Daytop Village are three exemplary treatment programs, models for many similiar facilities throughout the country. Unfortunately, many abusers and their families do not know where to turn for help. Ideally, school personnel, family physicians, and community health care workers can point people in the right direction. Also, many private volunteer organizations have set up clearinghouses for drug treatment information for the many people who are unfamiliar with the programs in their own communities. As more becomes known about centers such as those mentioned here, perhaps more funds and support will make it possible for greater numbers of substance abusers to seek out and receive help.

A mother comforts her child. It has been estimated that half of all babies born in the United States today will be using drugs by the time they are 15. In the 1980s, 40 percent of the population uses drugs.

CHAPTER 8

THE BOTTOM LINE

Despite all efforts at prevention and treatment, 70 million Americans regularly use illegal drugs. The statistics are staggering. Half of all babies born in the United States today will be using drugs by the time they are 15. Two-thirds of all high school seniors admit to using illegal drugs. Twenty years ago, fewer than 4% of Americans used drugs. Today the number of users is nearly 40% of the population.

Drug use figures significantly in the high rate of high school dropouts. It plays a major role in the rising death rate for people between the ages of 15 and 24. It leads to a large number of suicides, highway deaths, street crime, violence, child abuse, and divorce. The bottom line is that the United States has the highest level of drug abuse of any nation on earth.

Perhaps because of this sad truth, the efforts at prevention and treatment have been stepped up in recent years. Antidrug messages bombard the public from every direction. The American Association of Advertising Agencies has organized a massive campaign to fight drugs, using its own money and soliciting $1.5 billion in media space and time for antidrug advertising.

Business executive William O'Donell, a former drug addict, overcame his illness and went on to establish a rehabilitation center in Arizona. He is shown here hugging a patient at the center.

The Media-Advertising Partnership for a Drug-Free America is part of the largest task force ever assembled in the history of the communications industry. Its antidrug ads are being broadcast on TV and radio thousands of times a year. Hundreds of ads are in print in national magazines and newspapers.

Educators, politicians, and employers have also enlisted in the struggle. Every major school system in the country has added some form of drug abuse education to its standard courses of study. The federal government spends a billion dollars a year to enforce drug laws. Corporate managers and executives everywhere are calling the National Institute on Drug Abuse hot line, 1-800-843-4971, for help in setting up company drug treatment programs. This number is manned by Employee Assistance Program planners every weekday from 9:00 A.M. to 8:00 P.M..

The self-help groups and treatment centers discussed in this book — Phoenix House, Odyssey House, Women for Sobriety, the Betty Ford Center, Daytop Village, and their many counterparts — are in fact turning out many drug-free "graduates." These programs do not save lives. Rather, they provide an environment that enables people whose lives are at risk to save themselves. Every day they prove that drug addiction can be treated successfully. Addict after addict has been able to return to a life of dignity and pride no matter what degradation has gone before.

Unfortunately, for every addict who has gotten the message about substance abuse, acknowledged his or her addiction, and reached out for treatment, there are many more for whom drug use remains a way of life. Just as no one can predict with any certainty who will become addicted, no one can pinpoint which addicts will recover and which will not. Despite a number of impressive success stories, statistics show that addiction is one of the most intractable of all illnesses.

But every day, in treatment programs throughout the world, small battles are being won. Every day, as just one young person decides to say "no" to drugs, another small, but significant victory is recorded. The war on drugs will be waged for some time to come; it is up to both individuals and society as a whole to determine the ultimate outcome.

APPENDIX

State Agencies
for the Prevention and Treatment
of Drug Abuse

ALABAMA
Department of Mental Health
Division of Mental Illness and
  Substance Abuse Community
  Programs
200 Interstate Park Drive
P.O. Box 3710
Montgomery, AL 36193
(205) 271-9253

ALASKA
Department of Health and Social
  Services
Office of Alcoholism and Drug
  Abuse
Pouch H-05-F
Juneau, AK 99811
(907) 586-6201

ARIZONA
Department of Health Services
Division of Behavioral Health
  Services
Bureau of Community Services
Alcohol Abuse and Alcoholism
  Section
2500 East Van Buren
Phoenix, AZ 85008
(602) 255-1238

Department of Health Services
Division of Behavioral Health
  Services
Bureau of Community Services
Drug Abuse Section
2500 East Van Buren
Phoenix, AZ 85008
(602) 255-1240

ARKANSAS
Department of Human Services
Office of Alcohol and Drug Abuse
  Prevention
1515 West 7th Avenue
Suite 310
Little Rock, AR 72202
(501) 371-2603

CALIFORNIA
Department of Alcohol and Drug
  Abuse
111 Capitol Mall
Sacramento, CA 95814
(916) 445-1940

COLORADO
Department of Health
Alcohol and Drug Abuse Division
4210 East 11th Avenue
Denver, CO 80220
(303) 320-6137

CONNECTICUT
Alcohol and Drug Abuse
  Commission
999 Asylum Avenue
3rd Floor
Hartford, CT 06105
(203) 566-4145

DELAWARE
Division of Mental Health
Bureau of Alcoholism and Drug
  Abuse
1901 North Dupont Highway
Newcastle, DE 19720
(302) 421-6101

DISTRICT OF COLUMBIA
Department of Human Services
Office of Health Planning and
  Development
601 Indiana Avenue, NW
Suite 500
Washington, D.C. 20004
(202) 724-5641

FLORIDA
Department of Health and
  Rehabilitative Services
Alcoholic Rehabilitation Program
1317 Winewood Boulevard
Room 187A
Tallahassee, FL 32301
(904) 488-0396

Department of Health and
  Rehabilitative Services
Drug Abuse Program
1317 Winewood Boulevard
Building 6, Room 155
Tallahassee, FL 32301
(904) 488-0900

GEORGIA
Department of Human Resources
Division of Mental Health and
  Mental Retardation
Alcohol and Drug Section
618 Ponce De Leon Avenue, NE
Atlanta, GA 30365-2101
(404) 894-4785

HAWAII
Department of Health
Mental Health Division
Alcohol and Drug Abuse Branch
1250 Punch Bowl Street
P.O. Box 3378
Honolulu, HI 96801
(808) 548-4280

IDAHO
Department of Health and Welfare
Bureau of Preventive Medicine
Substance Abuse Section
450 West State
Boise, ID 83720
(208) 334-4368

ILLINOIS
Department of Mental Health and
  Developmental Disabilities
Division of Alcoholism
160 North La Salle Street
Room 1500
Chicago, IL 60601
(312) 793-2907

Illinois Dangerous Drugs
  Commission
300 North State Street
Suite 1500
Chicago, IL 60610
(312) 822-9860

INDIANA
Department of Mental Health
Division of Addiction Services
429 North Pennsylvania Street
Indianapolis, IN 46204
(317) 232-7816

IOWA
Department of Substance Abuse
505 5th Avenue
Insurance Exchange Building
Suite 202
Des Moines, IA 50319
(515) 281-3641

KANSAS
Department of Social Rehabilitation
Alcohol and Drug Abuse Services
2700 West 6th Street
Biddle Building
Topeka, KS 66606
(913) 296-3925

KENTUCKY
Cabinet for Human Resources
Department of Health Services
Substance Abuse Branch
275 East Main Street
Frankfort, KY 40601
(502) 564-2880

LOUISIANA
Department of Health and Human
  Resources
Office of Mental Health and
  Substance Abuse
655 North 5th Street
P.O. Box 4049
Baton Rouge, LA 70821
(504) 342-2565

MAINE
Department of Human Services
Office of Alcoholism and Drug
  Abuse Prevention
Bureau of Rehabilitation
32 Winthrop Street
Augusta, ME 04330
(207) 289-2781

MARYLAND
Alcoholism Control Administration
201 West Preston Street
Fourth Floor
Baltimore, MD 21201
(301) 383-2977

State Health Department
Drug Abuse Administration
201 West Preston Street
Baltimore, MD 21201
(301) 383-3312

MASSACHUSETTS
Department of Public Health
Division of Alcoholism
755 Boylston Street
Sixth Floor
Boston, MA 02116
(617) 727-1960

Department of Public Health
Division of Drug Rehabilitation
600 Washington Street
Boston, MA 02114
(617) 727-8617

MICHIGAN
Department of Public Health
Office of Substance Abuse Services
3500 North Logan Street
P.O. Box 30035
Lansing, MI 48909
(517) 373-8603

MINNESOTA
Department of Public Welfare
Chemical Dependency Program
  Division
Centennial Building
658 Cedar Street
4th Floor
Saint Paul, MN 55155
(612) 296-4614

MISSISSIPPI
Department of Mental Health
Division of Alcohol and Drug Abuse
1102 Robert E. Lee Building
Jackson, MS 39201
(601) 359-1297

MISSOURI
Department of Mental Health
Division of Alcoholism and Drug
  Abuse
2002 Missouri Boulevard
P.O. Box 687
Jefferson City, MO 65102
(314) 751-4942

MONTANA
Department of Institutions
Alcohol and Drug Abuse Division
1539 11th Avenue
Helena, MT 59620
(406) 449-2827

NEBRASKA
Department of Public Institutions
Division of Alcoholism and Drug
Abuse
801 West Van Dorn Street
P.O. Box 94728
Lincoln, NB 68509
(402) 471-2851, Ext. 415

NEVADA
Department of Human Resources
Bureau of Alcohol and Drug Abuse
505 East King Street
Carson City, NV 89710
(702) 885-4790

NEW HAMPSHIRE
Department of Health and Welfare
Office of Alcohol and Drug Abuse
  Prevention
Hazen Drive
Health and Welfare Building
Concord, NH 03301
(603) 271-4627

NEW JERSEY
Department of Health
Division of Alcoholism
129 East Hanover Street CN 362
Trenton, NJ 08625
(609) 292-8949

Department of Health
Division of Narcotic and Drug
  Abuse Control
129 East Hanover Street CN 362
Trenton, NJ 08625
(609) 292-8949

NEW MEXICO
Health and Environment Department
Behavioral Services Division
Substance Abuse Bureau
725 Saint Michaels Drive
P.O. Box 968
Santa Fe, NM 87503
(505) 984-0020, Ext. 304

NEW YORK
Division of Alcoholism and Alcohol
  Abuse
194 Washington Avenue
Albany, NY 12210
(518) 474-5417

Division of Substance Abuse
  Services
Executive Park South
Box 8200
Albany, NY 12203
(518) 457-7629

NORTH CAROLINA
Department of Human Resources
Division of Mental Health, Mental
  Retardation and Substance Abuse
  Services
Alcohol and Drug Abuse Services
325 North Salisbury Street
Albemarle Building
Raleigh, NC 27611
(919) 733-4670

NORTH DAKOTA
Department of Human Services
Division of Alcoholism and Drug
  Abuse
State Capitol Building
Bismarck, ND 58505
(701) 224-2767

OHIO
Department of Health
Division of Alcoholism
246 North High Street
P.O. Box 118
Columbus, OH 43216
(614) 466-3543

Department of Mental Health
Bureau of Drug Abuse
65 South Front Street
Columbus, OH 43215
(614) 466-9023

OKLAHOMA
Department of Mental Health
Alcohol and Drug Programs
4545 North Lincoln Boulevard
Suite 100 East Terrace
P.O. Box 53277
Oklahoma City, OK 73152
(405) 521-0044

OREGON
Department of Human Resources
Mental Health Division
Office of Programs for Alcohol and
 Drug Problems
2575 Bittern Street, NE
Salem, OR 97310
(503) 378-2163

PENNSYLVANIA
Department of Health
Office of Drug and Alcohol
 Programs
Commonwealth and Forster Avenues
Health and Welfare Building
P.O. Box 90
Harrisburg, PA 17108
(717) 787-9857

RHODE ISLAND
Department of Mental Health,
 Mental Retardation and Hospitals
Division of Substance Abuse
Substance Abuse Administration
 Building
Cranston, RI 02920
(401) 464-2091

SOUTH CAROLINA
Commission on Alcohol and Drug
 Abuse
3700 Forest Drive
Columbia, SC 29204
(803) 758-2521

SOUTH DAKOTA
Department of Health
Division of Alcohol and Drug Abuse
523 East Capitol, Joe Foss Building
Pierre, SD 57501
(605) 773-4806

TENNESSEE
Department of Mental Health and
 Mental Retardation
Alcohol and Drug Abuse Services
505 Deaderick Street
James K. Polk Building,
 Fourth Floor
Nashville, TN 37219
(615) 741-1921

TEXAS
Commission on Alcoholism
809 Sam Houston State Office
 Building
Austin, TX 78701
(512) 475-2577
Department of Community Affairs
Drug Abuse Prevention Division
2015 South Interstate Highway 35
P.O. Box 13166
Austin, TX 78711
(512) 443-4100

UTAH
Department of Social Services
Division of Alcoholism and Drugs
150 West North Temple
Suite 350
P.O. Box 2500
Salt Lake City, UT 84110
(801) 533-6532

VERMONT
Agency of Human Services
Department of Social and
 Rehabilitation Services
Alcohol and Drug Abuse Division
103 South Main Street
Waterbury, VT 05676
(802) 241-2170

VIRGINIA
Department of Mental Health and
  Mental Retardation
Division of Substance Abuse
109 Governor Street
P.O. Box 1797
Richmond, VA 23214
(804) 786-5313

WASHINGTON
Department of Social and Health
  Service
Bureau of Alcohol and Substance
  Abuse
Office Building—44 W
Olympia, WA 98504
(206) 753-5866

WEST VIRGINIA
Department of Health
Office of Behavioral Health Services
Division on Alcoholism and Drug
  Abuse
1800 Washington Street East
Building 3 Room 451
Charleston, WV 25305
(304) 348-2276

WISCONSIN
Department of Health and Social
  Services
Division of Community Services
Bureau of Community Programs
Alcohol and Other Drug Abuse
  Program Office
1 West Wilson Street
P.O. Box 7851
Madison, WI 53707
(608) 266-2717

WYOMING
Alcohol and Drug Abuse Programs
Hathaway Building
Cheyenne, WY 82002
(307) 777-7115, Ext. 7118

GUAM
Mental Health & Substance Abuse
  Agency
P.O. Box 20999
Guam 96921

PUERTO RICO
Department of Addiction Control
  Services
Alcohol Abuse Programs
P.O. Box B-Y Rio Piedras Station
Rio Piedras, PR 00928
(809) 763-5014

Department of Addiction Control
  Services
Drug Abuse Programs
P.O. Box B-Y Rio Piedras Station
Rio Piedras, PR 00928
(809) 764-8140

VIRGIN ISLANDS
Division of Mental Health,
  Alcoholism & Drug Dependency
  Services
P.O. Box 7329
Saint Thomas, Virgin Islands 00801
(809) 774-7265

AMERICAN SAMOA
LBJ Tropical Medical Center
Department of Mental Health Clinic
Pago Pago, American Samoa 96799

TRUST TERRITORIES
Director of Health Services
Office of the High Commissioner
Saipan, Trust Territories 96950

Further Reading

Alcholics Anonymous, Third Edition. New York: A. A. World Services, 1976.

Berger, Gilder *Addiction*. New York: Franklin Watts, 1982.

Brecher, Edward *The Consumers Union Report: Licit and Illicit Drugs*. Boston: Little, Brown, 1972.

Conrad, Barnaby *Time Is All We Have*. New York: Arbor House, 1986.

Hodgkinson, Liz *Addictions*. Wellingborough, England: Thorsons Publishing Group, 1986.

Hyde, Margaret O. *Mind Drugs*. New York: McGraw-Hill, 1981.

Long, Robert Emmet *Drugs and American Society*. New York: The H. W. Wilson, 1986.

Nelkin, Dorothy *Methadone Maintenance: A Technological Fix*. New York: Braziller, 1973.

Nellis, Muriel *The Female Fix*. Boston: Houghton Mifflin, 1980.

Phelps, Janice Keller, M.D., and Alan E. Nourse, M.D. *The Hidden Addiction and How to Get Free*. Boston: Little, Brown, 1986.

Woods, Geraldine and Harold. *Cocaine*. New York: Franklin Watts, 1985.

Worick, W. Wayne, and Warren E. Schaller. *Alcohol, Tobacco, and Drugs*. Englewood Cliffs, N.J.: Prentice-Hall, 1977.

Glossary

addiction a condition caused by repeated drug use, characterized by a compulsive urge to continue using the drug, a tendency to increase the dosage, and physiological and/or psychological dependence

Alcoholics Anonymous a self-help organization for the treatment of alcoholism and other addictions

alcoholism alcohol abuse causing deterioration in health and social relations

barbiturate a drug that has a depressing effect on the central nervous system and respiration; may have toxic side effects and when used excessively can lead to tolerance, dependence, and even death

behavior modification therapy a treatment for alcoholism that focuses on drinking as a learned behavior

Cannabis sativa the hemp plant

cocaine the primary psychoactive ingredient in the coca plant and a behavioral stimulant

cold turkey the sudden halt of use of an addictive drug

crack an adulterated, highly addictive form of cocaine

depressant a drug that depresses the central nervous system; used to help people block out unpleasant thoughts and anxieties and reduce tension

detoxification the process by which the body is rid of poisons or their effect

epidemic rapid spread or increase in occurrence affecting many individuals at one time

euphoria a mental high characterized by a sense of well-being

hallucinogen a drug that causes the user to see or hear things that are not there; LSD and peyote are examples of hallucinogens

herbicide a chemical agent used to kill plants

heroin a semisynthetic opiate produced by a chemical modification of morphine

methadone a synthetic narcotic administered orally to heroin addicts that satisfies the need for the drug without supplying the effects

morphine an opiate used as a sedative and pain reliever

Narcotics Anonymous a self-help group for drug addicts

nicotine a stimulant found in tobacco that causes dependence in habitual smokers

Odyssey House a New York–based treatment program that features a special residential program for addicted parents and their children

opiate compound from the milky juice of the poppy plant *Papaver somniferum*, including opium, morphine, codeine, and their derivatives (such as heroin)

opium a highly addictive drug prepared from the pods of the poppy plant

physical dependence adaptation of the body to the presence of a drug such that its absence produces withdrawal symptoms

psychological dependence a condition in which the drug user craves a drug to maintain a sense of well-being and feels discomfort when deprived of it

stimulant a substance that speeds up the activities of the central nervous system, increases alertness, and brings about a state of euphoria; crack, cocaine, and amphetamines are stimulants

tolerance a decrease of susceptibility to the effects of a drug due to its continued administration, resulting in the user's need to increase the drug dosage to achieve the effects experienced previously

withdrawal the physiological and psychological effects of discontinued use of drugs

Women for Sobriety a self-help program for women alcoholics

PICTURE CREDITS

Ad Council: p. 55; AP/Wide World Photos: pp. 36, 44, 46, 50, 53, 63, 65, 66, 68, 74, 82, 88, 92, 106; The Bettmann Archive: pp. 12, 39, 48, 49, 70; Daytop: pp. 103, 104; S. Farkas/World Health Organization: p. 27; W. A. Graham/United Nations: p. 60; John Isaac/United Nations: pp. 10, 84; Magnum Photos, Inc.: p. 110; New Life: pp. 75, 77; G. Palmer/United Nations: p. 108; Partnership for a Drug-Free America: p. 34; John Robaton/United Nations: p. 19; Catherine Ruello: p. 76; Mario Ruiz Picture Group: cover; P. S. Sudhakaran/United Nations: pp. 8, 33, 72; United Nations Photo: pp. 22, 40; UPI/Bettmann Newsphotos: pp. 20, 25, 26, 29, 30, 38, 42, 56, 58, 90, 94, 97; T. Urban/World Health Organization: p. 87

Index

Regina Avraham is the author of *The Downside of Drugs* in the ENCY-CLOPEDIA OF PSYCHOACTIVE DRUGS published by Chelsea House. She has been a science teacher with the New York City Board of Education since the 1960s. She also edits and writes textbooks for young adults, including her most recent, *Readings in Life Science* and *Readings in Physical Science.* Ms. Avraham presently teaches biology and general science.

Solomon H. Snyder, M.D., is Distinguished Service Professor of Neuro-science, Pharmacology and Psychiatry at The Johns Hopkins University School of Medicine. He has served as president of the Society for Neuroscience and in 1978 received the Albert Lasker Award in Medical Research. He has authored *Uses of Marijuana, Madness and the Brain, The Troubled Mind, Biological Aspects of Mental Disorder,* and edited *Perspective in Neuropharmacology: A Tribute to Julius Axelrod.* Professor Snyder was a research associate with Dr. Axelrod at the National Institutes of Health.

Barry L. Jacobs, Ph.D., is currently a professor in the program of neuroscience at Princeton University. Professor Jacobs is author of *Serotonin Neurotransmission and Behavior* and *Hallucinogens: Neurochemical, Behavioral and Clinical Perspectives.* He has written many journal articles in the field of neuroscience and contributed numerous chapters to books on behavior and brain science. He has been a member of several panels of the National Institute of Mental Health.

Joann Ellison Rodgers, M.S. (Columbia), became Deputy Director of Public Affairs and Director of Media Relations for the Johns Hopkins Medical Institutions in Baltimore, Maryland, in 1984 after 18 years as an award-winning science journalist and widely read columnist for the Hearst newspapers.